Designer Drugs

Paul R. Robbins

The Drug Library

ENSLOW PUBLISHERS, INC.

44 Fadem Road
Box 699
Springfield, N.J. 07081
U.S.A.

P.O. Box 38
Aldershot
Hants GU12 6BP
U.K.

This book is dedicated to Marguerite Horyna

Copyright © 1995 by Paul Robbins

Library of Congress Cataloging-in-Publication Data

Robbins, Paul R. (Paul Richard)
    Designer drugs / Paul Robbins.
        p. cm. — (The Drug Library)
    Includes bibliographical references and index.
    ISBN 0-89490-488-4
1. Designer drugs—Juvenile literature. [1. Designer drugs.
2. Drugs. 3. Drug abuse.] I. Title. II. Series.
RM316.R63 1995
362.29'9—dc20   94-16314
                                                   CIP
                                                       AC

Printed in the United States of America.

10 9 8 7 6 5 4 3 2 1

Photo Credits: Dr. David Nichols, p. 37; Dr. Lawrence Robbins, pp. 53, 59, 94; Drug Enforcement Administration, pp. 20, 28, 34, 71, 73; Fisons, p. 20;

Cover Photo: "©The Stock Market/Stanley Fellerman"

Acknowledgments

The author would like to thank Dr. Sharon K. Hauge and Daniel C. Robbins for their contributions to this book. He would also like to thank Dr. George Greer for his comments on the chapter dealing with the drug ecstasy. Grateful acknowledgment is also made to the following for permission to reprint excerpts from their copyrighted materials: Sussex Publishers, Inc. for M. Roberts, "MDMA: Madness, not Ecstasy," *Psychology Today*, June 1986; Plenum Publishing Corporation for R. Raskin, J. Novaceck, and R. Hogan, "Drug Culture, Expertise and Substance Abuse," *Journal of Youth and Adolescence*, 1992, pp. 21, 525–537; Franklin Watts for M. McCormick, *Designer-Drug Abuse*, 1989; The American Medical Association for T. Randall, "'Rave' Scene, Ecstasy Use, Leap Atlantic," *Journal of American Medical Association*, 1992, pp. 268, 1505–1506; and Ken Liska for *The Pharmacist's Guide to the Most Misused and Abused Drugs in America*, Collier, 1988.

Grateful acknowledgment is also made to the following organizations and individuals for providing the pictures used in the book: The Drug Enforcement Administration for the photographs of illegal laboratories (pp. 34, 71), Fisons, Biphetamine (p. 20), ice (p. 28), and drug seizure (p. 73); Dr. David Nichols of Purdue University for the photograph of ecstasy (p. 37); Dr. Lawrence Robbins of Michigan State University for the photographs on pages 53, 59, 94. Finally, the author would like to thank the National Clearinghouse for Alcohol and Drug Information for providing many resources that were helpful in writing this book.

Contents

Acknowledgments   3

Introduction   6

1 Characteristics of Designer Drugs . . .   9

2 MPTP and Speed 15

3 Ecstasy and the Fentanyl Analogs . . . 31

4 The Individual and Drug Abuse 46

5 The Family and Drug Abuse 56

6 Society and Drug Abuse 65

7 How to Get Help 77

Chapter Notes 97

Bibliography 103

Glossary 110

Index 111

Introduction

Some years ago I served as a consultant in a drug addiction ward of the Veterans' Administration Hospital in Washington D.C. While I was working on the ward, I carried out a number of research projects which gave me the opportunity to talk at length with many of the patients. Most of the patients had rather grim stories to tell. They told me about how they never thought they would become addicted to drugs when they first began to use them, but had indeed become so. They related how they stole to support their drug habits, became isolated from their friends and families, couldn't function on their jobs, and did time behind bars. As one patient put it, "I lost everything."[1]

Grim as their stories were, in a way, these patients were the lucky ones. They had not overdosed to the point of no return. They were alive to tell their stories. And, they were in a treatment program which offered hope for the future.

Not everyone is so lucky. One particular story, which appeared in a scientific journal published in Europe,[2] was about three young people, two of them nineteen-year-old men, the other, a seventeen-year-old girl. I can't tell you much about the young men or the girl. I don't know whether the girl was pleasant or talented or attractive. Researchers don't try to humanize things in research reports; they just present the basic facts.

One night at about 10:30, the three teenagers got together to use an illegal drug called methamphetamine. They were together in a room three stories above street level. It wasn't clear from the report whether they injected the drug into their veins or smoked it. It doesn't matter very much, because both methods send large quantities of methamphetamine to the brain very quickly.

Shortly after they began using the drug, the two men got into a heated argument. Sometimes methamphetamine brings on sudden, unpredictable, violent reactions. It is not usual, but it does happen. Upset by the argument, the girl went in search of help. When she returned with a friend, she found one of her companions dead on the floor. The amount of the drug that he had consumed was too much for him. If he had been a frequent user, he might have tolerated the drug. But, a heavy dose of methamphetamine for a novice user can be fatal.

The girl looked at her other companion. His behavior was bizarre. He was waving a kitchen knife in one hand and banging his head against the wall.

One can only imagine what the girl's reactions were at this point. One of her companions was dead; the other was out of his mind. It must have been overwhelming. She found a taxi and went home. By the time she reached home, she was very sick, and soon she collapsed. She was taken to the hospital, but the doctors could not save her. In two hours time, she died.

It is not clear from the report who witnessed the third act of this tragic story. But, this is what happened. The third member of this ill-fated trio had lost all sense of what he was doing. He leaped over the railing of the balcony that adjoined the room and plunged three stories to the ground. He died shortly afterwards from the injuries sustained.

Autopsies revealed the presence of methamphetamine in the blood of all three victims. It was not clear how much of the drug they had consumed, but it must have been a sizeable dose. The three victims had no idea that they would be using anything so potent. One wonders whether the dealer who sold them the drugs had any idea that this batch of drugs was lethal. Because of the slipshod way in which methamphetamine is often produced, the dealer may have been as much in the dark as the drug's victims.

You may have heard of overdose deaths from heroin or crack cocaine. The drug in this story was neither. On the street, it is called speed, crystal, ice, or half a dozen other names. It is not like heroin and cocaine, which come from plants. This one is made by chemists in a laboratory. It is one of a number of very powerful psychoactive drugs that are called "designer drugs."

If you are like most people, it is unlikely that you know exactly what the term designer drugs means. But, designer drugs are something you should know about. There may come a time when you will need to know.

1
Characteristics of Designer Drugs

Unlike a substance such as marijuana—whose history goes back to ancient times—designer drugs have only a brief history. The term "designer drugs" was coined in California, where the problems caused by these drugs were first observed. Gary Henderson, a University of California professor, has been credited with inventing the term. Henderson predicted that these drugs would be widely used on the streets, and he was right.[1]

There are many drugs of various kinds, both legal and illegal. What makes a drug a designer drug?

Designer drugs usually have several characteristics. First, designer drugs are synthetic. That is, they are not substances found in nature—they do not come from plants, such as marijuana is from canabis; heroin, from poppies; or cocaine, from the coca leaf. Designer drugs are made by people in the laboratory; they are newly engineered chemical compounds.

Second, since these drugs are made up from scratch, a person can try to design the drug to meet a specific need of the consumer—to give the consumer something that he or she wants. This goal of tailoring a drug to meet a need has nothing wrong with it. Pharmaceutical companies spend billions of dollars trying to develop drugs to meet specific medical needs, such as destroying cancer cells or controlling diabetes. If we can design drugs to do these things, so much the better for all of us.

It is a third characteristic that gives designer drugs their unsavory reputation. These drugs are not designed for use in medicine. Rather, they are designed to be very similar to drugs which are abused on the street, such as narcotics. By changing the chemical structure of a known drug in various ways, experimenters can come up with new drugs. These new drugs, called "synthetic analogs," are sometimes much more powerful than the original (parent) drugs they were based upon.

Models or diagrams can show how chemical compounds are altered to make new designer drugs. Take the drug fentanyl, a very important drug often used in surgery. If you look in a technical journal, this is how its chemical structure might be represented.[2]

To see how fentanyl is modified to make a designer drug which is sold on the street as China White, look for a moment at the second diagram.

$$\langle\bigcirc\rangle\text{-CH}_2\text{-CH-N}\langle\bigcirc\rangle\text{-N-}\overset{\overset{\displaystyle O}{\|}}{C}\text{-CH}_2\text{-CH}_3$$
$$\underset{\nearrow}{\text{-CH}_3}$$

At first glance, this diagram looks like a photocopy of the first diagram. If you look at the right side of the diagram, there is no change at all. But, if you look at the left side, you can spot one small change indicated by the arrows. In the first diagram, C, which stands for carbon, is attached to two hydrogen (H_2) atoms. In the second diagram, one of these hydrogen atoms has been replaced by CH_3, which is a methyl group. This modest change in chemical structure creates a very powerful illegal drug.

Of course, it is one thing to diagram a chemical and another to actually create it. How is a designer drug actually made? The instructions are not all that hard to find. They are available in scientific journals, in published books, and in recipes passed around from one underground chemist to another.

How many new drugs or analogs can be made from an existing drug? For some drugs, such as the narcotic fentanyl, there are hundreds of possibilities for spinning off new drugs.[3] This is of great concern to people who are trying to stop the problem of drug abuse in the United States, for they never know when a new designer drug may emerge on the streets.

For the most part, designer drugs are made by underground chemists. These are people who do their work illegally, often in makeshift laboratories. These chemists may or may not be well trained in chemistry. Once a person has the formula and equipment, it doesn't take a lot of knowledge about chemistry to get into the business of making designer drugs. These illegal operators have been called "kitchen chemists." They get into the business for one main reason: they can make a lot of money. There are many problems that may result from making drugs in these makeshift laboratories. Picture a group of people with little training, working with chemicals that have to be measured precisely and mixed thoroughly so that the drugs that are produced will all be the same strength. When you buy a bottle of aspirin tablets at the store, you know that each of the tablets will be about the same strength. If you buy a designer drug, you may find that one batch of the drug may have nothing in it but filler material (e.g., lactose or sucrose). In this case, the small amount of psychoactive ingredient normally used in making up the powder has been left out in the mixing process. In the uneven mixing process of the makeshift lab, the next batch may have much too much of the psychoactive ingredient. The unlucky person who buys this batch may overdose and die. Taking such pills is a risky business.

In the next chapters, we will discuss some of the designer drugs that have emerged on the streets during recent years. These drugs include MPTP, speed, ecstasy, and the analogs to the drug fentanyl. These analogs are sold on the street as heroin or synthetic heroin, often under the name of China White, a name given to a very pure form of heroin from Southeast Asia. We will talk about how these drugs were developed, what effects they have, and some of the risks they present to the user.

Questions For Discussion

1. Ask your pharmacist for the names of some synthetic (laboratory-made) drugs that are widely used in medicine. What do you think would be some of the advantages in making a drug synthetically?

2. Imagine that medicines used to treat high blood pressure, asthma, or other diseases were made under the same conditions that designer drugs are made. What thoughts would you have as a patient who might be using medicine made this way?

3. When a new designer drug appears on the street, what do you think might be some of the problems it would pose for physicians, police, and drug educators?

2

MPTP and Speed

MPTP, one of the most dangerous designer drugs, has an unusual, almost strange history. The story is in some ways like the tale of *The Sorcerer's Apprentice*, which was set to music by Paul Dukas and brought to the screen in Walt Disney's remarkable film *Fantasia*. As the Disney version unfolds, the sorcerer leaves his castle after instructing the apprentice to clean up the place. The apprentice soon tires of the job and begins to tinker with his master's magic to get the brooms, the buckets, and the water to do the job on their own. The tinkering creates a near disaster, almost drowning the apprentice in torrents of water. Only the timely return of the sorcerer saves the apprentice from doom.

For the central character in the real-life drama, unlike the Disney film, there is not such a happy ending. A twenty-three-year-old chemistry student at a California university had been using narcotics, but found, like many users, that there were risks involved in using illegal drugs.[1] He was concerned about the possibility of being arrested. To avoid this, he decided to put his knowledge of chemistry (which like the apprentice's knowledge of magic, was not up to the task) to work and make his own narcotics. He began making an analog of the painkiller meperidine. The compound he made was called MPPP. He was successful for about six months, and then disaster struck. While making one of his batches of MPPP, he unknowingly changed his procedure slightly. He probably used too much heat during the process and came up with something new, a compound containing MPTP. This is a neurotoxin, an agent that destroys brain cells and cripples people. MPTP creates symptoms very much like Parkinson's disease, a condition characterized by tremors, rigid muscles, a short-step shuffling walk, and difficulties in speaking.

As mentioned, the young man's story had a tragic ending. While under treatment for his disabling Parkinson's symptoms, he took an overdose of cocaine and died.

A team of physicians reported a similar case in Canada.[2] The patient had been under care in a hospital for eleven months, unable to speak above a whisper. He walked with a stooped, shuffling gait and was unable to feed himself. No one was quite sure what the problem was. Treatment with medications for Parkinson's disease finally brought him back to the point where he could talk about what had happened. He said he felt like he had been in a cage for the past months.

The patient admitted that he had been a longtime drug user. He said he had been snorting a homemade analog of meperidine daily for a week and then he was stricken with the disease. He stopped talking and eating and became withdrawn and was sent to a psychiatric hospital. The patient reported that he had made the compound many times before—but this time something had gone wrong. Some of the ingredients he used had become discolored. A chemical analysis of powder found in his home showed that it contained the neurotoxin MPTP.

It would be nice to say that these are medical curiosities or isolated incidents, but they are not. Hundreds of cases were reported during the 1980s, many in California.[3] These stories bring the old saying to mind, "A little knowledge can be a very dangerous thing."

Speed

Speed is one of the street names for methamphetamine. We have encountered speed already in our discussion in the introduction of the three young people who overdosed on the drug. If you look at the word "methamphetamine" and cover up the first four letters, you can see right away that the drug is a member of the amphetamine family.

In some ways, the effects of amphetamines on a person resemble what happens when he or she is facing a stressful situation. Imagine for a moment that you are in a risky situation . . . that someone is threatening you with physical harm or you are driving a car that is out of control, or even imagine that you are giving a speech before the class and you feel nervous about it. When a person is in a situation that is stressful, the body mobilizes to meet the emergency in what has been called "a fight or flight reaction." Adrenaline is released into the bloodstream. Breathing becomes faster. The heart beats faster. Blood pressure increases. The person is primed and alert. Amphetamines are man-made drugs that produce some of these reactions. There are

17

bodily reactions such as increased blood pressure and mental reactions such as increased alertness. The drugs have other effects as well. Amphetamines fight off fatigue and elevate mood. All amphetamines are "psychostimulants"—drugs that increase the activity of the brain. Some college students who have partied too much instead of studying have used these drugs to stay awake in last-minute cramming for an exam.

Benzedrine™ and Dexedrine™ are two of the more familiar names for amphetamine. These drugs can be legally prescribed by physicians for certain medical problems. These pills come in doses of five to ten milligrams. Abusers of these drugs take them in large numbers.

In an interesting article, John P. Morgan and his colleagues summarized the history of amphetamines.[4] Amphetamine first appeared in 1931 as an over-the-counter drug. Anybody could buy it: No prescriptions needed, no questions asked. The drug was used in nasal sprays as a decongestant. If people wanted to take something to relieve a stuffy nose, they could go to a pharmacy and ask for Benzedrine™. Try doing that today and you may get a very funny look from the pharmacist. You might also find drug enforcement agents checking up on you.

Even in this early form as a decongestant, its users began to notice the drug's phsychoactive effects. Some users took the spray bottle apart and removed the paper which contained 250 milligrams of amphetamine. These paper strips were sometimes consumed in chewing gum or mixed into a beverage.[5]

In time, it was noticed that people who took the drug had poor appetites. They just didn't seem to be as hungry as they were before taking the drug. Physicians took advantage of this effect and began to use amphetamine in the treatment of people who were overweight. This may not have been such a good idea, because the drug lends itself to abuse. People develop tolerance for amphetamine. They need higher and higher doses to get the same effect. Because of this problem, physicians are now advised to be very cautious about using the drug for weight control.

Fisons, a drug manufacturer which made an amphetamine called Biphetamine™, suggested that the drug be used for only a few weeks in weight reduction.[6] If tolerance occurred, the dose was not to be increased. Rather, use should stop.

Another use of the drug has been to control the behavior of hyperactive children. You may have known children who are restless, always moving about and who can't seem to concentrate on anything for very long. Amphetamine has been used to quiet down these children. You wouldn't think the drug would work for this purpose because it is a stimulant—yet it often does.

Children were given small doses of the drug. Fisons suggested a starting dose of five milligrams of Biphetamine™, once or twice daily for children six years of age or older. The dose could be gradually increased. Fisons reported that it was rarely necessary to go beyond forty milligrams per day.

As you might imagine, giving amphetamine to young children has stirred up controversy. Many people feel uneasy about using such a drug to modify the behavior of children. They see too much potential for abuse and would prefer to try other ways to deal with the problem such as counseling and behavior modification techniques.

During World War II, both the United States and its enemies gave amphetamine to combat soldiers. It is easy to see how tempting it would be to take a pill to keep alert if you were on a long bombing mission over enemy territory or keeping

While it seemed unlikely that a stimulant would be effective in calming hyperactive children, Biphetamine™ was sometimes used in small doses for this purpose.

watch in a convoy of ships in waters patrolled by enemy submarines.

In small doses, amphetamine increases alertness and fights off fatigue. In large doses, these drugs will bring on a feeling of euphoria. The users experience a psychological lift, a sense of well-being. People who wanted to get high from chemicals began to use these drugs. Large quantities of the drugs began to be diverted from medical use onto the street. Drugs were stolen from the manufacturing plants, trucks, pharmacies, and even from physicians. Finally laws were passed to regulate the flow of these drugs. The government's crackdown made these drugs much less available.

Methamphetamine—Quick and Potent

Methamphetamine—a member of the amphetamine family—was discovered many years ago by a Japanese chemist but did not emerge into public awareness until the 1960s. In the 1960s, an injectable form of the drug hit the streets. The drug popularly known as "speed" was also called by such names as "crank," "go-fast," "shabo-shabo," "glass," "go," and "zip." Speed was not only abused in the United States, it became a problem in other countries such as Japan and Korea as well.[7] An important fact about speed is that the chemical gets into the brain quickly. As the National Institute on Drug Abuse (NIDA) describes it, "Methamphetamine enters the brain more rapidly than other members of the amphetamine group, because it is more soluble in the brain's membranes, thereby producing a 'rush' of euphoria when injected or smoked."[8]

Even small doses of speed may produce feelings of excitement. Speed decreases appetite and increases blood pressure and heart rate. NIDA notes that "Users report a 'pounding heart' sensation, palpitations, hot flashes, dryness of the mouth, and sweating."[9]

Methamphetamine can not only be injected into the blood stream but can also be smoked. While current users are much more likely to inject the substance than smoke it, this could well change. Injection of any substance poses the risk of contaminated needles and the possibility of picking up HIV, the infection that causes AIDS. In addition, there have been reports from Oregon that some people injecting speed have developed acute cases of lead poisoning.[10] As for smoking speed, some Japanese abusers have devised a simple way of doing it. They heat the substance on aluminum foil and inhale the smoke with a straw or paper pipe. When smoked, the effect of the drug has been reported to be milder than when injected.[11] Still, smoking speed is an efficient way of delivering large quantities of the drug to the brain. The psychoactive effects are quickly experienced.

Compared to a drug such as cocaine, the effects of speed are long-lasting. C. Edgar Cook of North Carolina's Research Triangle Institute observed that "Cocaine levels after smoking, rapidly peak and . . . also rapidly decline with a terminal half-life of about fifty-six minutes . . . Methamphetamine levels, although they rapidly approach peak concentration, remain high for a considerable period before declining with a half-life of about eleven to twelve hours."[12] What this means is the concentration of the drug in the blood only decreases by half in eleven to twelve hours time after it has been absorbed. The effects of the drug on the body and mind will persist for many hours.

As is true for legally prescribed amphetamines, continued use of speed produces tolerance. The chronic user has to increase the dose to obtain the effect he or she has come to expect. NIDA notes that some abusers may increase their dose "50 to 100 times the initial amount over time, up to several hundred milligrams per day, which would be fatal to the nonuser."

What are the effects of such high doses? NIDA lists these as mental confusion, severe anxiety, aggression, tremors, chest pain, heart irregularities, convulsions, and death. Some chronic high dose users experience a drug-induced psychosis. They may experience delusions of persecution and hallucinations; they believe people are out to get them and they hear things that aren't there. There are reports that some drug users have the sensation that there are bugs and parasites in their skin. They then begin picking at their skin.[13]

One of the sobering thoughts about the use of speed is that heavy use of the drug can lead to permanent brain damage. It is important to realize that damage caused by the drug to the nerves in the brain cannot be reversed. The fact that at high doses speed can be very dangerous is attested to by statistics collected at hospital emergency rooms. In 1988, in a group of selected hospitals, there were over three thousand emergencies in which speed was part of the problem.[14]

Once a person becomes a regular user of speed, it becomes hard to quit. Stopping the drug brings on unpleasant withdrawal symptoms such as depression, decreased energy, and the inability to experience pleasure. These symptoms are accompanied by an intense craving for the drug.

The use of methamphetamine can be detected in a number of ways. It is possible to detect the substance in blood samples, urine samples, and even in hair samples.

Amphetamines and Aggression

We mentioned that NIDA has linked amphetamine use to aggressive and sometimes violent acts. Since most people do not become aggressive after using these drugs, it becomes important to better understand the conditions under which amphetamine use leads to aggression. Klaus Miczek, who has been doing research on this question has made some interesting observations. He notes that these aggressive effects seem to occur "in really aggressive people who have taken amphetamines for a long time." He goes on to explain, "Let me give you an example of this, which is particularly true in homicides. The individual is engaged in an activity and suddenly misinterprets something. He wakes up in the back of a car and smells poison gas and hits someone over the head with a pipe wrench. Or he is robbing a store and someone smiles. There is a sudden impulse and he kills the individual. If you look at the court records, you see the story repeatedly. . . ."[15]

Miczek notes that these violent incidents seem to be dose related. At low doses, amphetamines may have a calming influence on aggressive children. So, Miczek sees three factors that may make a difference in whether amphetamines trigger a violent episode: whether a person is prone to be aggressive, how long the person has been using the drug, and the dose of the drug.

Amphetamine abuse has been implicated in a number of murder cases. During a Japanese epidemic of amphetamine abuse, it was noted that in a two-month period, thirty-one out of sixty convicted murderers had some association with amphetamine abuse.[16] Researcher Everett Ellinwood, Jr. has

24

interviewed a number of convicted murderers in the United States for whom amphetamine pills or speed seemed to play a role in the homicide. Reporting his observations in *The American Journal of Psychiatry*, Ellinwood noted that in some cases, the dose of the drug used was huge.

The case of Mrs. C. illustrates what can happen with very high doses of amphetamines.[17] Mrs. C. had a number of psychological problems before she ever began to use amphetamines. She was lonely and depressed. She was given amphetamines by a physician as a way to help her lose weight. While taking the drug, Mrs. C. found that the pills made her feel better. She began to use them to relieve her depressed feelings. Tolerance to the drug developed, and she gradually increased her dose to 400–600 milligrams per day. At this high dose level, she began to experience hallucinations.

Mrs. C. entered into an affair while her husband was out of the country for an extended period. When she knew her husband was about to return, she told her lover that they would have to break up. At the same time, she became extremely jealous of her lover's possible interest in any other women.

Her emotions went through swings and she began to pop amphetamine pills continuously. She reached the point where she was using as much as 1,200 milligrams per day. In a turbulent mental and emotional state, she saw her lover for the last time. When she told him that she was going to leave for good, he responded by teasing her that he would bring his new girlfriend by her home. Angered, she replied that she would kill him. Pulling out a pistol from her waistband, she shot him several times. Her mental state had been so ravaged by the drug that she told a bystander to turn the body over and take a photo of his pretty face. While she was being questioned at the police station, she remarked she would have to leave for a hairdresser's appointment. Months later when she was interviewed, she was rational, outgoing, and friendly. The amphetamine-induced psychosis was gone; but, the harm it had done could not be undone.

Users' Perceptions of Amphetamines

Some of the things that researchers have learned about speed have been discussed . . . what they have discovered from laboratory, clinical, and statistical studies. You have seen some of the things speed does for the user and sometimes to the user. You might wonder, what do the users, themselves, think about speed? Do they find using the drug a positive experience? Do they recognize the dangers involved?

A study was carried out in the Veterans' Administration Hospital in Washington D.C., which relates to these questions.[18] Patients in a drug treatment program who had used amphetamines either in the form of speed or pills were asked to assess their reactions to the drug. They were asked to use a technique called the semantic differential. The technique asks the subjects to react to an object—in this case, a drug—in terms of word pairs like "good-bad," "sharp-dull," and "heavy-soft." The subject makes these ratings on a seven-point scale. In the first word pair example given, seven represents something that is clearly good; one, clearly bad. In the study, we asked patients to rate amphetamines and two other drugs (heroin and marijuana) on fourteen word pairs that have an evaluative flavor.

The figure on the next page presents the average (mean) ratings for the group of patients for each of the fourteen word pairs for amphetamine. As you scan the figure, you can see that most of the ratings are closer to the positive words than for the negative words. Obviously, these patients liked using the drug.

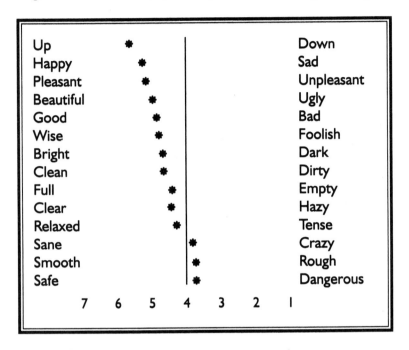

Up		Down
Happy		Sad
Pleasant		Unpleasant
Beautiful		Ugly
Good		Bad
Wise		Foolish
Bright		Dark
Clean		Dirty
Full		Empty
Clear		Hazy
Relaxed		Tense
Sane		Crazy
Smooth		Rough
Safe		Dangerous

7 6 5 4 3 2 1

Did the patients see any negatives? There were a few. The use of amphetamines was closer to rough than smooth, crazy than sane, and dangerous than safe. While most of the users saw the drug in a positive light, they recognized that there are hazards involved.

"Ice": Methamphetamine's New Look

In recent years, methamphetamine has been given a new form. Instead of powder, the drug comes in the form of a large, clear, very pure crystal that is smoked in a glass pipe. The street name for this form of methamphetamine is "ice" or "crystal."

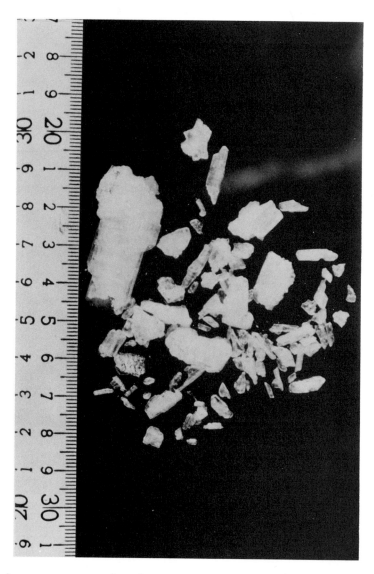

In recent years, methamphetamine has taken a new form. Instead of a powder, the drug now comes in the form of a large, clear, very pure crystal that is smoked in a pipe. The street name for this new form of the drug is ice or crystal. If you were to look closely at the crystals, you would see that they resemble ice or crystal formations.

Ice became a problem in the late 1980s. Ice is a dangerous drug that some users can really get hooked on. In discussing the use of ice, Marissa Miller reported some findings from interviews that had been carried out with heavy users in Hawaii who had entered drug treatment.[19] Miller noted that these heavy users would "binge" (repeatedly use) the drug. This binging "typically would entail continuous use for an average of five days, during which time they would forego both food and sleep. Between binges, users reported extensive sleeping or what they called 'crashing out.' The time between binges was reported to be approximately three to four days for most users interviewed." These ice abusers were either smoking the drug or sleeping it off. By the time they entered treatment, the rest of their lives had nearly vanished.

Questions For Discussion

1. Have you ever known a person who was using amphetamine under a doctor's prescription? If so, what were the medical reasons for this use? Did you notice any effects of the drug on the person's behavior?

2. Speed stays active in one's system for many hours. Can you think of any added hazards that this long-lasting effect might present?

3. Some ICE users in Hawaii have reported a pattern of binging on the drug for days at a time, sleeping, then binging again. What would such behavior do to the user's ability to hold a job, perform in school, or be a responsibile parent?

3

Ecstasy and the Fentanyl Analogs

There's something in a name. If you were walking down the street at night and someone emerged from the shadows and said, "Hey, do you want to buy some 3,4-methylenedioxymethamphetamine?" you would probably react by shaking your head. "Who needs that?" you might think, "Whatever it is." But, if the voice in the shadows had used the word "ecstasy" instead of that tongue-twisting chemical name, a different picture might have entered your mind. "Ecstasy" suggests a most wonderful experience, something like spending time at the beach with the girl or boy of your dreams or gazing at the earth from an orbiting spacecraft. Some very shrewd drug dealers found that they could sell a lot of pills with a name like "ecstasy."

Ecstasy, also known as MDMA, XTC, and Adam, was developed by a German company in 1914 about the time the First World War broke out. The company apparently planned to

31

market the drug as an aid in dieting, but soon gave up the idea. Like an old clock ticking away, the drug sat on the shelf, and the patent for the drug expired.

Ecstasy is a good example of a designer drug. Ecstasy (MDMA) is made in the laboratory, altered from an existing synthetic drug called MDA. Both MDA and MDMA are chemically similar to speed. In his book on widely-abused drugs, Ken Liska notes that MDA first appeared on the streets of San Francisco in 1967. The mid-and late 1960s were very unsettled times in the San Francisco Bay area. With the backdrop of an unpopular war raging in Vietnam, hippies gathered together in the streets, students protested at the universities, and many young people went out of their way to reject the traditional values of American society. Drug use was part of this "counter-culture."

Liska notes that when MDA appeared on the streets, it was well regarded. The drug produced "a sensual, easily managed euphoria." Liska referred to MDA as the "Mellow Drug of America."[1] As time passed and MDA became less popular, it was replaced on the street by MDMA. The drug that had been ignored for so many years now had a new life.

Ecstasy is a powder that may be taken orally in the form of a pill or capsule. Liska notes that a dose of 50 to 150 milligrams would be an "effective hallucinogenic dose."[2] Scientists studying the effects of ecstasy have tended to use doses toward the higher end of this range. In one study, inexperienced users were given 75–150 milligrams of the drug. In another study carried out on people who had used the drug a number of times, the subjects picked their own dose levels and these averaged about 150 milligrams.[3] When MDMA is bought on the street, buyers have no way of knowing what dose they are getting, or even whether they are buying pure MDMA.

The reason for this uncertainty is that the ecstasy produced in the United States is often made in small scale operations with little attention to quality control. These illegal labs have been set up in garages, kitchens, and mobile trailers. The drug makers have used such rinky dink procedures as setting up chemical reactions in cookie jars and removing solid products with coffee filters. Analyses of ecstasy samples sold on the street have revealed they are often contaminated with other substances.

The Effects of Ecstasy

What does ecstasy do? Does it live up to the promise of its name? Users of the drug report that it does create a feeling of euphoria.[4] Users also report that while taking the drug, their attention is focused on the here and now, instead of the past or future. These effects are not long lasting, typically fading within three hours. The positive mood the person experiences, however, may linger on. Users of the drug also report heightened sensual awareness.

People taking the drug in the company of others have reported that they feel closer to the other people present. They say that they communicate better and that they feel more loving. So far, the effects of the drug sound quite positive. We should point out, however, that some of these psychological effects, such as feeling closer to others, may be due to the situation in which the person uses the drug and not to the action of the drug itself. When people come together in a positive social setting and "expect" to feel better after taking a drug, they are likely to feel better even if the drug used is a placebo—a substance that looks and tastes like the real thing, but isn't. Being in good company

This make-shift lab is typical of the small-scale operations used to produce ecstasy and other designer drugs. With little to no attention to quality control, the drugmakers can often unknowingly contaminate the drugs they produce in these labs.

and having expectations that pleasure will be experienced can be powerful influences on the way a person thinks and feels. Until research has ruled out these effects, we have to be cautious about accepting all of the claims made for ecstasy.

Even if future research makes it clear that ecstasy does have the positive psychological effects that users claim, we still must ask, "Is there a downside to using this drug? Are there undesirable effects?" The answer is that there are several. First, some people who take the drug get nauseated. Instead of becoming euphoric, they just throw up their last meal. Second, many people find their jaws tensing and their teeth clenching while using the drug. This problem sometimes lasts for hours after the drug has worn off. Third, the pulse and blood pressure increase. These increases pose a risk to someone with high blood pressure or heart problems. Fourth, at times users experience unwanted, undesirable psychological reactions. NIDA has listed confusion, depression, sleep problems, severe anxiety, and paranoia among the psychological difficulties that may occur "during and sometimes weeks after taking MDMA."[5]

Sometimes, the anxiety brought on by ecstasy may become a full-fledged panic reaction. Some cases of panic reactions following the use of ecstasy are described in an article in *Biological Psychiatry*.[6] One of the cases involved Mr. N., a 27-year-old salesman who had been a frequent user of the drug (about twenty times during the previous ten months). One day he drank two pints of beer and consumed fifty milligrams of MDMA. Suddenly he became tense. His heart began to palpitate and his palms became sweaty. The room began to spin. He experienced trouble breathing and he became afraid he was going to die. He had to be treated in a hospital. After he was released, he quit both drugs and alcohol. The panic attacks still continued twice a week. Further medical treatment was successful in stopping the attacks.

At times, reactions to MDMA may be bizarre. Researcher Ronald Siegel has observed "When doses are pushed, we get madness, not ecstasy." Siegel also said, "I've seen people get ecstatic, and I've seen people crawl into fetal positions for three days."[7]

Medical journals contain examples of these unusual reactions to ecstasy. In *The British Journal of Psychiatry*, there are accounts of a young man and a young woman who had bizarre reactions to the drug.[8] The man had been brought into the hospital after jumping into the path of ongoing cars. During the clinical examination, he reported that he had been using ecstasy four to seven times a week for several months. His girlfriend reported that he had been behaving in an eccentric manner, walking around the apartment nude, uttering incoherent speech. He stated that people were out to kill him. The second case was about a twenty-two-year-old woman who had used ecstasy twice. After she took the drug, she reacted by thinking she was God and was dancing with the devil. She also experienced visual illusions of people with contorted faces. For a period of time after she stopped taking the drug, she experienced flashbacks of these contorted faces.

While such odd reactions to MDMA are far from typical, people must be aware that using any psychoactive drug is an uncertain venture. The user never can be quite sure what is going to happen.

Perhaps, what is most troubling about ecstasy are research studies on animals indicating that the drug can damage nerve

Ecstasy, shown here in its crystallized form, has been shown in animal studies to cause damage to the nerve cells in the brain. Because of this and a wide variety of other problems, it is considered a dangerous drug, and has been placed on the government's list of controlled substances.

cells in the brain. This may bear on findings reported on a small sample of long-term human MDMA users: They showed mild to moderate impairment of memory in psychological testing.[9] In studies carried out on animals being given high doses of MDMA, researchers have found that the drug has been shown not only to cause nerve damage, but also to decrease a vital chemical called serotonin. It is used to transmit messages in the brain. Serotonin is one of the key chemicals the brain uses in regulating mood. Many people who feel very depressed have low serotonin levels.[10] While studies on MDMA and serotonin have been lacking on human subjects, the results from the animal studies argue strongly against using the drug.

Because of these problems, MDMA is considered a dangerous drug and is on the government's list of controlled substances. Producers and sellers of the drug are subject to fines of up to $125,000 and fifteen-year prison terms. The drug seems to be most popular with college students and young professionals. A study carried out in 1987 at Stanford University revealed that 39 percent of the undergraduates had tried the drug. The areas of the United States in which MDMA use is highest include California, Texas, Florida, New York, and the New England states.

Ecstasy and Rave Parties

Like speed, ecstasy is not simply an American problem. Ecstasy has become a problem in many countries. There are reports of ecstasy abuse in Australia, Spain, and in the British Isles. Ecstasy has been quite popular in England, where the drug has been widely used as a "recreational drug." It has been estimated that one-half million people in England have used ecstasy.[11]

In the late 1980s, ecstasy use in England became associated with a new fad, "rave parties." Rave parties are all-night dance sessions, sometimes held in clubs where crowds of people "mosh." When British authorities clamped down on these drug-using parties, the concept was exported to the United States with some souped-up features added. Writing in *The Journal of the American Medical Association,* Teri Randall described these rave parties.

> *Staged in empty warehouses or open fields outside San Francisco or Los Angeles, their parties are drawing thousands of young Californians on designated weekend nights.*
>
> *Party goers—attired in "Cat in the Hat" hats and psychedelic jumpsuits—pay $20 at the door to dance all night to heavily mixed, electronically generated sound, surrounded by computer-generated video and laser light shows. They pay another $3 to $5 for "smart drinks"—amino acid-laced beverages that reputedly enhance energy and alertness. And for another $20, those so inclined can purchase an ecstasy tablet.*[12]

While it sounds like a good-time-seeker's ultimate experience, these parties sometimes turn out to be more than the person bargained for. In England, the combination of ecstasy pills and prolonged, vigorous dancing has done some unexpected things to the human body. At least fifteen young people have died. Their body temperatures soared to as high as 110 degrees. Their blood pressures fell sharply. Some developed acute kidney failure.

Death followed in two to sixty hours after hospital admission. Why this happened is still something of a medical mystery; but, there may be something about combining the drug with frantic activity that is potentially lethal. We know that driving and alcohol don't mix. It may be that dancing and this drug don't mix either.

A final note about ecstasy is that the drug may not lend itself well to steady use. Ecstasy users have reported developing a tolerance to the positive effects of the drug, while the undesirable effects seem to worsen with continued use.

Fentanyl Analogs

If you bought one of these synthetic analogs on the street, you would probably be told you were buying China White. China White is a mysterious name, calling up images of far away places . . . something out of the Orient, something remote or exotic. But, China White possesses beauty only in name. What it is, is very pure heroin from Southeast Asia—an addictive narcotic.

Fentanyl analogs are often sold on the street as China White. The buyer may or may not be told that the drug isn't real heroin. Chances are the buyer wouldn't know the difference. It looks like the real thing and, depending on the dose, acts like the real thing. The only difference is the potential effects. The fentanyl analogs are much more powerful drugs.

The fentanyl analogs were created from a very useful drug. The parent drug fentanyl was developed by the Janssen Pharmaceutical Company of Belgium. Fentanyl is widely used as an anesthetic in surgery. Chances are that if you have had surgery in recent years, you have been given fentanyl. It has been estimated that 70 percent of all operations in the United States are carried out with the aid of this drug.[13]

We said that fentanyl is powerful. To be more precise, fentanyl is about one hundred times more potent than morphine. The duration of effect for the drug is relatively short.

With one exception, the parent drug fentanyl has not lent itself to illegal use. The exception is an interesting one and involves horse racing. Because the action of fentanyl is short-lived and the presence of the drug is very hard to detect in routine chemical analyses, the drug was used to dope (excite) horses before a race.

Incidentally, one of the fentanyl drugs has been used to temporarily immobilize animals in the wild. You may have seen nature shows on television in which scientists use darts to immobilize animals in order to place radio transmitters on them so they could study their movements in the wild. The drug used could well have been carfentanyl.

A variety of illegal designer drugs based on fentanyl have appeared on the street—and some of these are even stronger than the original drug. The first drug to appear on the streets, alpha-methyl fentanyl, is two hundred times as potent as morphine. A later drug, 3-methyl fentanyl is about three thousand times as potent as morphine![14] You can imagine what that might do to the user.

Fentanyl analogs are usually injected, though they can be smoked or snorted. Robert J. Roberton, who was chief of California's Alcohol and Drug Programs, noted that if you touched a batch of the substance, it might feel like fine powder. He compared the texture of the drug to powdered milk. But, he also observed that not all batches of the drug feel the same.

Sometimes, the powder feels coarse and will crumble in one's fingers. Fentanyl analogs have no particular odor that can help the users identify them. Roberton stated that there is "nothing characteristic about the appearance of any sample that will identify it as fentanyl."[15]

If a drug dealer said he was selling heroin and it was really fentanyl, it is unlikely that anyone would be able to tell the difference by looking at it or touching it. Heroin users, who have been victims of such substitutions have sometimes paid for it with their lives.

How difficult it is for even the most experienced heroin users to tell just what it is they are actually getting when buying China White was illustrated in testimony before the Senate Subcommittee's hearing on designer drugs. A thirty-eight-year-old male who had been in treatment for heroin addiction for many years noted that a new batch of higher quality heroin had shown up on the streets of Baltimore, where he lived, and nobody knew what it was. He reported that there had been "quite a few overdoses," and he knew someone who had died. He suspected it might have been a designer drug. "So, I think they are in Baltimore. And the problem is we are not sure what they are. There are no labs that can test for that in the area." He said he couldn't tell by the price. Synthetic heroin sold at the same price as real heroin. Nor would the dealer level with the users. "What they are doing is misrepresenting it as 'China White' heroin or 'Mexican Brown' . . . and they are using all kinds of cutting agents—you can make 'Mexican Brown' by putting instant coffee in it, and cutting it up, and it will turn brown."[16]

Let's talk about what these fentanyl analogs do. First, they are narcotics and act like narcotics such as morphine and heroin. When a person takes the drug, he may feel a sense of euphoria. This high occurs within a few minutes of taking the drug. Also, the drugs are powerful painkillers. Fentanyls depress breathing. This effect has a short duration; breathing is usually normal in fifteen to thirty minutes. Depending on the dose given, the drug will slow down the user's pulse by as much as 25 percent. If the normal pulse is seventy-two, a person might find himself with a pulse of fifty-four, which is on the low side. The blood pressure is also likely to fall considerably. At high doses, the user may also experience some tightness in the chest as muscles become more rigid.

Like heroin, fentanyl users will develop tolerance for the drug. Like heroin, the drugs are physically addictive. The addicted user will experience withdrawal symptoms when he or she does not have a supply of the drug available.

An overdose of these drugs can be fatal. In 1985, Roberton noted that over one hundred deaths caused by an overdose of fentanyls had already taken place. Most of the victims were white males who lived in California. Later reports indicate fatalities from fentanyl analogs have spread to other states. Writing in a 1991 issue of the *Journal of the American Medical Association*, Jonathan Hibbs and his colleagues reported a number of deaths in Pennsylvania that involved overdoses of fentanyl analogs.[17] The potential for these drugs to become a very serious problem is very real.

There are ways of treating an overdose of a fentanyl analog in hospital emergency rooms. The emergency room staff strives to maintain the user's vital signs and that may require resuscitation. The attending physician will probably administer the drug

Naloxone, which blocks the action of narcotics. You can imagine the scene in the emergency room in which the staff is administering the drug every two to three minutes, watching intently for a response.[18]

People who overdose on fentanyl analogs are probably better off if there is someone around who can tell the emergency room staff exactly what happened. Fentanyl analogs are very difficult to detect in routine laboratory tests. If the emergency room team must deal only with an unconscious patient, it may take time before the attending physician can be certain that he or she has correctly diagnosed the problem. Time with an overdosed patient can be very important.

Questions For Discussion

1. Do you think the street names given to drugs, for example, "ecstacy", or "china white" make a person think that a drug is more exotic than it really is?

2. Some ecstasy users say that the drug makes them feel closer to other people. Could you design an alternative drug-free approach to acheiving this goal? You might include such things as teaching people to become more sensitive listeners, sharing activities, and showing that they care.

4

The Individual and Drug Abuse

We have discussed some of the designer drugs that have appeared on the streets in recent years: MPTP; speed or, in its new smokeable form, ice; ecstasy; and the fentanyl analogs that sell under names like "China White." While these drugs differ from one another in various ways, they have at least two things in common—they are illegal, and they are dangerous. They are all on the U.S. government's list of controlled substances. And yet, large numbers of people use one or more of them.

Why do people use drugs that could do them serious harm, even kill them? It is not an easy question to answer. We know that most people never use illegal drugs of any kind. We know that other people use drugs at times, but never make a habit of it. Drugs never become an essential part of their lives. And, we know that still other people become heavy users of drugs and many of these users become addicted. For some people, like those ice-addicted patients in Hawaii, there is nothing much left in life but drugs.

When we ask why people differ in their willingness to use drugs and in their response to them, the answers are complicated. However, research is beginning to give us some insights into the problem. And this is important—for the more we understand why people use or do not use drugs, the more likely it is that we will be able to come up with drug prevention programs to help stop drug abuse before it starts and develop effective treatment programs for those who are hooked on designer drugs and want to stop.

In this and the next two chapters, we are going to explore the question of why people differ in their willingness to use designer drugs. In our discussion, we will consider four types of possible explanations. The first has to do with heredity: Is there any evidence that heredity plays a role in drug abuse? Is there something in a person's genes that sets him or her up, increasing the chances of developing a substance abuse problem? The second type of explanation is psychological. What are the motivations for drug abuse, and what role do our individual personalities play in getting involved with drugs? Thirdly, we will look at the role of our families. What is it about family life that increases or decreases our chances of becoming substance abusers? Finally, we will look at the role of the larger society in both contributing to and dealing with the problem of drug abuse.

Genes and Drug Abuse

Each of us inherits from our parents the genes that shape and influence the way we develop as human beings. Genes determine our physical appearance; have a strong influence on our intelligence; and to a lesser extent, influence the way we behave. Do genes influence the likelihood of our becoming substance abusers? Researchers tell us it is unlikely that we will find a single gene or a combination of genes that causes a person to become a drug abuser. What might turn out to be the case is that genes have some influence, either directly or indirectly on why one person is more likely than another to use drugs if the opportunity presents itself. It is also possible that genes influence the way a person will react when taking drugs. Genetic differences may also shed some light on why some people are able to control their use of drugs, while others become addicted.

It should be clear that we are not looking for a one-to-one correspondence between genes and behavior. If a person has any genetic tendency towards substance abuse, it does not necessarily mean that he or she will become a substance abuser. Imagine a world in which there were no substances to abuse. In such a world you would never know if you had an increased genetic risk of abusing drugs because there would be no substances to abuse. If you never use drugs, you will never become addicted.

Researchers use several methods to explore the possibility that there is a genetic basis for a medical or behavioral problem. One method is to see whether a problem "runs in families." If you had a condition like allergies to weeds and grasses and your parents had them, and your brothers, sisters, and grandparents had them, it would certainly look like the condition had a hereditary basis. A second technique is the twin study. Identical twins have exactly the same heredity. They have identical sets of genes. Non-identical twins—children born together, but who do not look alike—share the same number of genes as any other pair of brothers and sisters. If behavior such as substance abuse has a genetic basis, we would expect to find identical twins more alike in their use of drugs than non-identical twins. The third method is adoption studies. If a parent has a condition (such as allergies), and the child is separated from the parent at birth and raised in a different environment and yet develops the condition, we would suspect a hereditary basis for the problem. A change in environment didn't seem to matter that much.

It is interesting that many heroin users have alcoholic parents and that sometimes more than one heroin user is found in the same family. Researcher Edward Kaufman noted that he treated a family for heroin addiction where the father and four of the five children were heroin addicts.[1] However, we should not jump to the conclusion that the addiction was transmitted through the genes. A person can easily become involved with drugs by simply observing and modeling the behavior of other family members who use a drug. I have worked with families in which several children were using drugs and the parents were clean. The children learned drug use from each other.

Research, to date, linking heredity and drug abuse has been limited and inconclusive. At this point, there is some evidence which suggests that genes may play a role in substance abuse, particularly alcohol, but we can't yet be sure as to whether this extends to the drugs sold on the street, including designer drugs. We have to keep an open mind on this. As scientists are studying the problem, it shouldn't be too long before we have better information.

Psychological Aspects of Drug Abuse

There is a basic principle in psychology. Acts which are reinforced tend to be repeated.[2] The principle is not absolute, but it is a pretty good rule of thumb. If you talk to drug users, they can usually tell you something that is reinforcing about using drugs. Take marijuana, for example. Using a questionnaire, I asked marijuana users, "Now please tell us in your own words what it is like to smoke marijuana. How would you describe the feelings and sensations you experience?" Some typical responses were "very relaxed, happy feelings, erotic," "relaxation-release from stress," and "relaxation and a certain degree of intensified emotions be it hilarity, sensitivity, warmth or whatever."[3] *Now it is certainly true that not all reactions to the drug were positive. Some people reported feeling depressed and insecure. Still, the reactions to using the drug were on the whole positive—and as long as the experience was reinforcing, the tendency was to repeat the act.*

Users tend to view other drugs as reinforcing, too. Recall the positive terms in which users viewed amphetamines. The drugs were rated closer to beautiful than ugly, pleasant than unpleasant, and happy than sad. Or take ecstasy. In her book, author Michelle McCormick cited a user's response to ecstasy.

> *It's very beautiful and can show a person a lot, like psychedelics . . . it shows people avenues of their self that they never even thought of before. Where psychedelics open the mind, MDMA opens the heart. And you get into stuff like universal love.*[4]

This kind of reaction would motivate the user to experience these feelings again. Even the drugs that get people into the deepest difficulties have their reinforcing elements. Some heroin addicts whom I interviewed spoke of the drug in very positive terms. So, when we ask why people use drugs, we can't ignore the reinforcing qualities of these drugs. They can be very powerful.

Clearly, not everyone reacts the same way to drugs. It seems reasonable that people who experience very positive reactions to drugs and few negative ones would be the people most likely to cross the line from drug use to drug dependency. And, indeed, a study carried out by John Schafer and Sandra Brown on college students has shown that for both marijuana and cocaine, the highest level of drug use was associated with expectations for positive drug effects.

A negative reaction to drug use such as a panic reaction or depression is likely to put a damper on drug use—at least temporarily. In discussing ecstasy and its tendency to nauseate some users, Ronald Siegel noted that if someone took a drug promising ecstasy, and it made him throw up he wouldn't be likely to take it again.[5]

There is a clue in the responses of the marijuana users that points out another aspect of the motivations for illegal drug use. The users talked about "relaxation" and "release from tension." The implication is that drug use for some people serves as a technique for coping with stress.

Stress is common in modern life. We all experience it at times. Some of us feel under a lot of stress much of the time. There are many ways to cope with stress. A few examples are trying to do something about the problems that are producing stress, seeking the company of friends or family, and trying to escape from the problems, at least for a while. Some people, however, use drugs to cope with stress. In doing research on coping techniques, we found that some people cope with the discomforts of stress by trying to "narcotize" the unpleasant feelings away.[6] They rely on alcohol, drugs, and even sex to ease their discomfort. The relief obtained is temporary. When stress returns, what then? You can see the seeds of a drug dependency problem.

The motivations for using drugs appear to change somewhat as children grow older. Typical reasons offered by middle school pupils for using drugs are to relieve depression, to escape from problems, to satisfy curiosity—to see what effect the drugs would have—to relax, and to have a good time. High school drug users add heightening sexual pleasure to their list, and college students add expanding consciousness. Interestingly, research suggests that boys are more likely to report that they use drugs for pleasure, while girls tend to use drugs as a way of coping with distress.[7]

Personality differences also play a role in whether a person becomes involved with drugs. Here are a few of the personality traits or patterns that researchers have identified which appear to be associated with increased risk of becoming a substance abuser.[8]

Impulsivity. This is a tendency to act without thinking. If the idea pops into a person's mind to do something, he just goes ahead and does it without giving much attention to the consequences.

Autonomy. This is a person's need to do things his own way, a need to be independent and free. This can lead to self expression and creativity which are positive. It can also lead a person to experiment with drugs.

Less emphasis on achievement. Some people don't value achievement highly. They take a short term, rather than a long

This middle school encourages its students to be drug-free. Since the motivation for using drugs such as designer drugs seems to change somewhat as children grow older, it is best to try and prevent the use from ever beginning.

term, perspective. They may develop a mind set of "Why delay gratification today for some goal in the distant tomorrow?"

Risk taking. Some people buy and sell stocks. Some gamble in casinos. Some people skydive from airplanes. Some try drugs such as ice or ecstasy.

Alienation. A person who is basically turned off by the society in which he or she lives is a good candidate for drug abuse. In its extreme form, alienation takes the form of not caring about oneself or anyone else. The deeper a user drifts into the drug scene, the more hardened these feelings may become.

Questions For Discussion

1. What are your own theories about why young people abuse designer drugs?

2. Designer drugs can have serious side effects. Judging from the poeple that you know, how likely is it that information about these side effects would stop most people from trying these drugs?

3. One of the reasons that many young drug users give for using drugs is relaxation. What are some other non-drug-related forms of relaxation that you can name?

5

The Family and Drug Abuse

I am going to draw sketches of two families that are very much like families I know or have worked with in my clinical practice. The first family, the Howards, is an example of a family that seems to work well. The household is well organized. The parents manage things well. All the family members seem to know what they are supposed to be doing and what is expected of them. The rules governing the children's behavior are clear and consistent. Conversation between Mr. Howard and Mrs. Howard is usually civil and respectful. They seldom raise their voices at each other and rarely get into heated arguments. Both parents spend as much time as they can manage talking with their children. Both parents are affectionate with their children. The Howards teach the traditional values of hard work and self-reliance. They expect a lot of their children. They encourage and reward excellence in school.

The Clark family is about as different from the Howards as it can be. While most everything works well in the Howard family, nothing seems to go right for the Clarks. Meals are hit or miss. Cleaning and chores are often left undone. There is little togetherness. When the family does get together, it is often unpleasant. Both Mr. and Mrs. Clark are prone to heavy drinking. When they drink, they often become hostile. They seldom have anything good to say about each other or to each other. They beat on each other with words, and sometimes they get physical. The children have had their share of being slapped around too, and usually they avoid the house. The children's behavior is seldom supervised. The parents show little interest in the children's schoolwork and rarely make an effort to help them.

Now one can't say with certainty that the Howard children will stay out of trouble—including drug abuse—or that the Clark children will get into trouble and abuse drugs. Many children overcome early problems and do very well in life. And even the best parenting provides no guarantee that children will not at some time become drug abusers. The reach of parents in today's society is limited and drug abusers have come from all sorts of families. Still, if we wanted to place a bet on which children would be more likely to get into trouble and begin to use drugs, we would have to bet on the Clarks.

Social scientists have found that the way the family functions is a pretty good predictor of whether the child will experience later problems such as delinquency and drug abuse. Families that are disorganized, have ineffective ways of managing things, and lack clear rules, are more at risk for problem behavior.[1]

Psychologists have carried out many studies on parenting

and the way it influences children's problem behaviors, including drug abuse. A recent example would be a study of African-American and Puerto Rican adolescents in New York City. The researchers led by Judith Brook found that a close, mutual attachment between parents and children made a difference in whether the children became involved with drugs. When parents were perceived as warm, when children "identified" with their parents, when the relationship was low on conflict—these things seemed to help bolster children's resistance to using drugs.

In an article reviewing the research on parent-child relationships and drug abuse, David Hawkins and his associates noted the importance of parents remaining actively involved in their children's daily activities. They observed that when parents are not close to their children, are not involved in their activities or schoolwork, or are lax or inconsistent in discipline, this pattern of non-involvement or worse, indifference, often lays the groundwork for future problems.[2] When parents don't have the time or act as if they don't care, the child is more likely to venture into risky and sometimes self-destructive pathways.

Simply having an open line to a parent can make a difference in whether a child becomes a drug user. In studying teenagers, researchers Randy Kafka and Perry London found that the presence of open lines to at least one parent was associated with lower levels of all substance abuse, including designer drugs.

An emphasis in the family on negative communication is no help either. In studying the families of adolescent drug abusers, researchers have found that the communication patterns are often negative. There are heavy doses of criticism and blaming and little in the way of praise.

Researchers report less drug use among students who are involved in extracurricular activities. It is also extremely important that parents stay closely involved with their teens' activities. This closeness between teens and their parents has also been shown to lessen teen involvement with drugs.

This is the soil in which many kinds of social and psychological problems will develop and flourish—not just drug abuse. One of the things that gives substance abuse a big push is the use of alcohol or drugs in the home. The abuse of alcohol or drugs by parents makes it seem like a natural part of growing up—of becoming an adult.

Children develop their attitudes toward substance use in much the same way they develop their attitudes toward other things in life. They see what their parents are doing, they talk with their friends, and they watch television. If the parents smoke, the children are much more likely to tell researchers that they intend to smoke also. One researcher reported that having a parent who smoked doubled the chances that the child intended to smoke.[3] The same pattern is true for alcohol. If the parents drink, the children are more likely to say that they too intend to drink. Researchers have reported that as the number of family members who use alcohol increases, so do the child's chances of stating that he or she intends to drink.[4] And consider these statistics for marijuana. When no one in the household used marijuana, only 4 percent of the children questioned said they used or intended to use it. A single user in the family changed this number to 23 percent. Two users changed it to 39 percent.[5] When parents use drugs, children often will too. This is natural enough, because children tend to model what their parents do. Parents are older and more experienced.

The studies we have just cited suggest that it is not only the parents who set an example of using or not using drugs. The behavior of older brothers and sisters is important too. Some researchers use statistics based on the number of family members that includes brothers and sisters. And, indeed, researchers have reported that the presence of older brothers or sisters in the home who use drugs increases the risk of the younger child using drugs.[6]

What the family members do is important in communicating attitudes about drug use. What they say is also important. The values passed on in the house make a difference. Consider the attitudes expressed in the home about substance use. Take smoking as an example. We mentioned that having a parent who smokes doubles the chances of a child deciding he wants to smoke. Now, if the parents also convey the attitude to their children that smoking is okay, the chances not only double that the child will want to smoke, they may quadruple.[7]

Traditional values like those of the Howard family act to help avoid substance abuse. In a review of research on adolescent drug use, Diana Baumrind noted that frequently, a traditional upbringing shields children from early exposure to drugs.

As parental control lessens during adolescence, the values learned in the home will have to stand on their own if a teen is to resist pressure from peers to begin using drugs. If a child thinks long-range in terms of a future career, sees education as the road to get that career, has learned to enjoy activities which are not drug-related (e.g., sports, dancing, music, using the computer), and has developed a sense of personal responsibility, the odds are that child will not be easily persuaded by the urgings of drug-using peers. Strong family ties and extracurricular activities are often associated with resistance to drugs.[8]

How much pressure will children feel to experiment with drugs? It depends in part on the people the child hangs around with. Research has shown that friends who use drugs increase the risk of a child experimenting with drugs. Friends who are achievers decrease the risk.[9]

We have observed how family life lays the groundwork for experimentation with drugs or avoidance of drugs. Clearly many young people will decide to experiment with drugs, usually alcohol, and sometimes marijuana. While most young people who try these gateway drugs will never go beyond them, some will begin using cocaine, heroin, speed, or other designer drugs. In time, they may become drug dependent and in many instances, physically addicted. Few of these people will ever seriously think that they will become addicted until they wake up one day and find that they are.

When a person develops a psychological dependency or physical addiction to drugs, the problem often rebounds back on the family. First, many drugs are expensive. For example, ice, the crystal form of very pure methamphetamine, is very expensive. In Hawaii, a 1990 report put the cost of a gram of ice at between $300 and $400.[10] You could buy a new monitor for your computer or spend a few days vacationing at the beach for that much.

Where does a person get the money to support a designer drug habit? If someone is addicted to designer drugs, he or she may do some unbelievable things to get that money. Many people who are addicted to designer drugs end up stealing money from their families. Some begin a life of crime, such as selling drugs to other people. A large number of them are arrested.

People who are heavily involved with designer drugs may drift into a pattern of deception with their families. Questions of "Where have you been?" and "What have you been doing?" are not likely to bring an honest answer if the son or daughter has been buying and using designer drugs. Patterns of evasion, deception, and outright lying are common with drug abusers. The bonds of trust within the family are gradually lost. In some cases, they snap. You can imagine the reactions of many parents when the truth of the drug abuse problem comes out.

Hard-core drug addicts tend to drift into a life which is at odds with society. Their circle of friends becomes other addicts. They often become alienated from their families and feel depressed. Interviews of ice abusers in treatment in Hawaii revealed that most of the clients (85 percent) had experienced negative effects on their family life.[11] Seventy-nine percent reported such effects on their social life and 73 percent on work or school performance. These figures are similar to what we previously reported on heroin abusers.[12]

Many designer drug abusers never realize what they are getting into when they begin to use these powerful addictive drugs. They do not really believe that they will become controlled by designer drugs. They say they can control the use of the drug. These illusions are only shattered when their lives are shattered. Some never recover. The lucky ones get into treatment and try for a new beginning.

Questions For Discussion

1. Why do you think parents' involvement with their children's activities tends to reduce the risk of their children experimenting with drugs?

2. What effects do you think drug abuse by parents has on their children? What effects do you think drug abuse by children has on their parents?

3. Researchers have reported that an open line of communication between parent and child is associated with a smaller chance that the child will abuse drugs. What steps do you think parents and children can take to make sure that such open communications exist?

6

Society and
Drug Abuse

When you have a headache, what do you do for it? Do you just put up with it until it goes away, or do you reach into the cabinet where there are bottles of pills—some new, some which have been sitting there seemingly forever—and take something? There are a number of effective medicines which will lessen pain, and it can become the most natural thing in the world to toss that pill into your mouth, wash it down with a glass of water, and continue with your day.

If you have an upset stomach, you can take a pill to settle it. There are pills to take which can stop a runny nose, decongest a stuffed up head, put a person to sleep when he or she can't fall asleep, and lessen a person's anxiety when he or she feels jittery.

Americans take millions upon millions of pills every year. Some medicines are clearly needed. Insulin can be the difference between life and death for a diabetic. Antibiotics can wipe out dangerous infections. Other medicines are very useful in helping people cope with a variety of chronic problems, such as arthritis and allergies. Still other medicines, for many of us, are more like conveniences, controlling the pains and discomforts of daily life. Think of some of those pills in the medicine cabinet, pills which can relieve the temporary discomforts we all experience.

The message that you can relieve discomforts and feel better by taking a pill is repeated every day in the mass media. Think of some of the ads that you have seen on television for medicines to relieve headaches, "the minor pains" of arthritis, upset stomach, skin problems, hemorrhoids, and insomnia. If you watch a lot of television, you may be able to recite some of the commercials word for word.

The messages are clear, repetitive, and effective. How hung up is America on feeling good through chemicals? Here is a statistic. Draw your own conclusions.

"By 1962, the legal production of amphetamines was estimated by the Food and Drug Administration to be more than 8 billion tablets per year . . ."[1]

While the message to take legal, over-the-counter drugs is heavily advertised in the mass media, the message to use illegal drugs, such as designer drugs, is passed by word-of-mouth and by example. In some areas, you may see people buying drugs on the street or using drugs. Friends, associates, even family members may urge someone to use drugs. These activities are part of an underground culture, popularly called "the drug culture."

In recent years, we have heard a lot about the drug culture and designer drugs. We see the drug world in the movies and on television; we read about it in the newspapers and hear about it on radio talk shows. When we speak of the drug culture, we are talking about a kind of subculture within the larger society where buying, selling, and using designer drugs is a large part of everyday life. The drug culture has its own language and its own set of rules. It is an illegal but very real part of present-day society. Designer drugs invade our streets, neighborhoods, and schools. Drug dealers reach out and try to recruit the young. In the District of Columbia, researcher Patricia Bush found that by the time children were in the seventh grade, one out of every six questioned had been approached to sell drugs.[2]

In such an environment, children pick up information about street drugs at an early age. Robert Raskin and his colleagues tested over two thousand children in Tulsa, Oklahoma, in regard to their knowledge about drugs. They asked questions about the street names of drugs, the relative cost of different drugs, and the effects of these drugs. The researchers concluded that ". . . many youth know about drug culture as early as the sixth grade. Moreover, the reliability of this knowledge increases over time." The researchers indicated that drug knowledge in the middle grades was fragmented, consisting of bits and pieces of unrelated information. But, by high school, knowledge about drugs was well organized. "By the tenth, eleventh, and twelfth grades, information about drug use reflects a coherent domain of knowledge . . ."[3]

Many teenagers know a good deal about drugs. They have seen the ads promoting over-the-counter products. They know a lot about illegal street drugs, such as designer drugs. Much of what they have heard is that taking drugs makes you feel better. However, there is another side to the issue, and they have heard this too. They hear messages in drug education programs that drugs are harmful. They see posters stating that there are better things to do than use drugs, and the smart thing is to just say "NO!" Drug education messages are presented in the schools, on radio and television, and in talks by celebrities and athletes.

At times, the messages that drugs will make you feel better and that drugs are harmful may seem conflicting, if not confusing. What makes one drug good and another drug bad?

First, it has to be made clear that even very useful drugs prescribed by physicians or sold over-the-counter have possible "adverse effects." A drug as useful as aspirin can upset your stomach while curing your headache, and some people are allergic to aspirin. Medications should be used carefully. It is a good idea to check with your physician or pharmacist if you have any questions.

There should be no problem telling the difference between a useful drug such as an antibiotic and a dangerous drug like a fentanyl analog sold as China White. An antibiotic may save your life. The fentanyl analog might take it. But, what do you say to someone who complains, "My father drinks three martinis before dinner, and he gets mad when I smoke pot. It's no worse than what he does." Or what about, "My mother has a prescription for amphetamines. What's wrong with me for using speed? I don't see any difference." My answer would be that drugs sold on the street are illegal, of uncertain quality, and can have adverse effects. We have discussed the adverse and sometimes dangerous effects of designer drugs at length. Even when amphetamines are obtained with prescriptions, physicians are often very concerned, because it is far too easy to step over the line from use to abuse with these drugs.

If society contributes to drug abuse by promoting chemicals

as quick fixes for discomfort, society also pays a big price for the results. Most of us are familiar with the problems caused by heroin and cocaine. The problems caused by designer drugs have not been as well publicized as those caused by heroin and cocaine, but they are very real and of growing concern.

Methamphetamine (speed, ice) has been a particular problem. The drug puts people into emergency rooms of hospitals, and as such puts a further strain on this overworked part of our health care system. While the numbers have not been huge, there are more than enough cases to "make the charts" kept by the government's monitoring system for emergency rooms. The problem has been especially serious on the West Coast and in Hawaii.[4]

Another problem caused by speed is its abuse by drivers of motor vehicles. For men and women who have to drive long hours, the use of amphetamines is a seductive idea. A study was carried out on what truckers think about the use of speed and other drugs. A survey revealed that a majority of truckers believed that at least 20 percent of their fellow truckers drive while using illegal drugs, including speed.[5] Now we don't know how close this perception is to reality, but a large number of drivers using drugs is a disturbing idea when we think about safety on our highways.

When there are accidents on the nation's railroads, the Federal Railroad Administration routinely performs drug and alcohol testing on employees. Employees are checked not only for amphetamines, but for a number of other drugs as well.[6]

The way speed is manufactured presents a number of safety and environmental problems. Some of the chemicals (phosphine, ethanol, and benzene) used in the production of the drug are highly flammable. Other chemicals (sodium, potassium metals, and magnesium) react with water or air and may ignite or explode. It has been reported that about one-third of the designer drug laboratories uncovered by the police in Oregon were found after on-site explosions.[7]

Underground designer drugmakers are not always careful about the way they mix their products. They may be equally careless about the way they dispose of these chemicals. Gary Irvine, an environmental health supervisor in the state of Washington, and NIDA's Ling Chin have noted that these "solvent chemicals may be dumped into the ground or into sewers or septic systems, thus contaminating surface water, ground water, and wells, requiring extensive cleanup efforts."[8]

The increasing numbers of underground designer drug laboratories in the United States pose a problem not only to public health officials, but also to law enforcement officials. In 1981, there were eighty-eight laboratories seized by law enforcement agents. By 1989, the number had risen to 652.[9] That is a 600 percent increase! To this date, most of the illegal laboratories have been in California, but the numbers are rising in other states as well. Texas and Oregon are among the states with higher numbers of underground laboratories that have been shut down.

If this upward trend continues, a very large problem will emerge. If the efforts to slow the flow of heroin and cocaine into this country succeed, and it becomes harder to obtain these drugs on the street, we would only have to look within our borders to see an alternative underground designer drug industry growing. This would probably result in thousands of illegal laboratories, loaded with dangerous chemicals. They could be staffed by poorly trained workers, producing drugs of uncertain, unknown

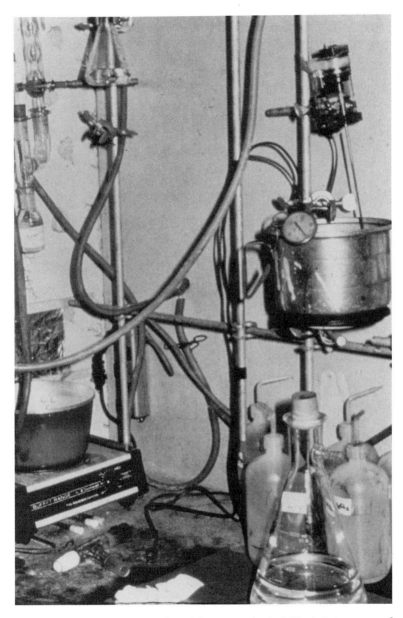

This underground designer drug laboratory made LSD. It is just one of the hundreds of illegal laboratories that United States drug authorities are now trying to shut down. But, with new illegal labs popping up everyday, it is virtually impossible to do away with all of them.

quality to be sold on American streets. And when we get tired of speed, ecstasy, and the current fentanyl analogs, what will be the next designer drug spun off from existing chemicals? The situation may remind you of the story of Pandora's box. Now that the lid is off, we may be seeing difficulties for many years.

These difficulties may be already upon us. In the state of Michigan, people have begun to use a designer drug called methcathinone or "CAT." According to a recent article in *Drug Abuse Update*,[10] the use of CAT has already spread to the neighboring state of Wisconsin. This designer drug was developed in Great Britain as an anti-depressant and diet aid (sound familiar?—remember the history of ecstasy?), but because it was addictive, it was not marketed. In time methcathinone found its way to Russia, where its use left many people addicted. The drug later surfaced in northern Michigan.

CAT can be used in a variety of ways—snorted, injected, or mixed with beverages. The drug is very potent and leaves the user feeling energized. *Drug Abuse Update* reports that many users binge on the drug, ignoring eating and sleeping, and that these binges may lead to both physical and psychological distress. Among the problems mentioned are weight loss, fatigue, irritability, depressed feelings, and at times, violence.

CAT is risky to make and produces toxic waste in the environment. As is true for other designer drugs, it is illegal to manufacture CAT or distribute it. The penalties for violating the law can be severe, but that is unlikely to stop some would-be manufacturers, for there is a lot of money to be made in producing designer drugs. The manufacture of designer drugs offers fertile ground for those who are interested in making big bucks and are indifferent to the harm they will cause to others.

With the street value of designer drugs far greater than the amount of money required to produce those same drugs, it is unfortunately quite an enticing business for many people today. The DEA task force is shown here making an arrest in a drug distribution case.

In 1985 testimony before the United States Senate Drug Enforcement Administration, Chief John C. Lawn placed the financial gains of underground designer drug makers in perspective. In speaking of fentanyl analogs, he remarked, "It is estimated that one kilogram of a fentanyl analog, which is equivalent to as many as 50 million dosage units, could be manufactured for less than $2,000. The street value of this quantity of fentanyl analogs would be more than one billion dollars."[11]

Today, we are dealing with a serious problem that is taking its toll in wasted lives. We must try to prevent an explosion of the problem that could create another drug abuse nightmare in future years.

Questions For Discussion

1. Americans consume billions of pills each year to relieve headaches, stomach aches, stuffy noses, and other symptoms. Imagine what it would be like if none of these pills existed and we lived like our ancestors, without the benefit of these modern remedies. How would you cope with the aches and pains of everyday life in a society without pills?

2. What are some of the things that you like about the drug education programs in your school? What suggestions would you have to improve these programs?

3. With the possibility that people will use speed or other drugs, then drive, would you be in favor of routine drug testing for airline pilots or operators of buses and trains?

7

How to Get Help

If you are a young man or woman who has been using speed or ice at higher and higher doses and are beginning to worry about what might happen—where do you go for help? If you are a person who has been using any dangerous designer drug and are beginning to appreciate the risks involved, you may be thinking "I've got to stop this. What do I do?" It is not easy for most people to stop using powerful psychoactive drugs. Like many others, you may need help. And if you do, where do you turn?

If you use drugs of any kind, you may be saying to yourself "I don't need to read any further, because I really don't need any help. I don't have that big a problem, and besides I can handle it myself." That may or may not be true. If you are a steady user of designer drugs, you may have passed the point where you can effectively deal with drugs on your own. In any event, it is certainly better to ask for help before you *have to* get help.

There are articles in *Postgraduate Medicine*[1] and *The Journal of Emergency Medicine*[2] which give advice to doctors on how to treat people who are rushed to emergency rooms overdosed on designer drugs. At that point, things get difficult and the outcome may be uncertain. For methamphetamine overdose there is no specific antidote.[3] The hospital staff must do the best it can with supportive care. The effects of some designer drugs like the fentanyl analogs are so powerful that the drug user may not reach the emergency room alive.

Where can someone find help? One of the best places to begin searching for a drug treatment program is within the pages of a very thick paperback book entitled *The National Directory of Drug Abuse and Alcoholism Treatment and Prevention Programs.* The book contains a state-by-state, community-by-community listing of thousands of drug and alcohol abuse treatment centers. The book gives names, addresses, phone numbers, and in some cases, hotline numbers. Single copies of the directory are available in limited numbers by writing to the following address:

The National Clearinghouse for Alcohol and Drug Abuse Information

P. O. Box 2345
Rockville, Maryland 20852.

If you would rather begin by talking to someone in your own state, you can telephone or write your state office of substance abuse. The following pages contain names and addresses provided in the 1993 *National Directory of Drug Abuse and Alcoholism Treatment and Prevention Programs.*

STATE AUTHORITIES

Alabama
J. Kent Hunt, Acting Director
Division of Substance Abuse Services
Department of Mental Health and Mental Retardation
200 Interstate Park Drive
P.O. Box 3710
Montgomery, AL 36193
(205) 270-4650

Alaska
Loren A. Jones, Director
Division of Alcoholism & Drug Abuse
Alaska Department of Health & Social Services
P.O. Box 110607
Juneau, AK 99811-0607
(907) 465-2071

American Samoa
Fualaau Hanipale, Assistant Director
Social Services Division
Alcohol & Drug Program
Government of American Samoa
Pago Pago, AS 96799
(684) 633-4606

Arizona
Terri Goens, Program Manager
Office of Substance Abuse
Division of Behavioral Health Services
Arizona Department of Health Services
2122 East Highland
Phoenix, AZ 85016
(602) 381-8996

79

Arkansas
Joe M. Hill, Director
Arkansas Bureau of Alcohol and Drug Abuse Prevention
108 E. 7th Street
400 Waldon Building
Little Rock, AR 72201
(501) 682-6650

California
Andrew M. Mecca, Dr. P.H., Director
Governor's Policy Council on Drug & Alcohol Abuse
1700 K Street, 5th Floor
Executive Office
Sacramento, CA 95814-4037
(916) 445-1943

Colorado
Robert Aukerman, Director
Alcohol and Drug Abuse Division
Colorado Department of Health
4300 Cherry Creek Drive, South
Denver, CO 80222-1530
(303) 692-2930

Connecticut
Susan Addiss
Commissioner
Connecticut Department of Public Health & Addiction Services
999 Asylum Avenue, 3rd Floor
Hartford, CT 06105
(203) 566-4145

Delaware
Neil Meisler, Director
Delaware Division of Alcoholism, Drug Abuse and Mental Health
1901 North DuPont Highway
Newcastle, DE 19720
(302) 577-4461

District of Columbia
Maude R. Holt, Administrator
DC Alcohol and Drug Abuse Services Administration
1300 First Street, N.E., Suite 325
Washington, DC 20002
(202) 727-1762

Federated States of Micronesia
Eliuel K. Pretrick, MO, MPH
Department of Human Resources
P.O. Box PS70
Palikir, Pohnpei FM 96941
(691) 320-2643

Florida
Pamela Peterson
Deputy Assistant Secretary
Alcohol and Drug Abuse
Florida Department of Health & Rehabilitative Services
1317 Winewood Blvd.
Building 6, Room 183
Tallahassee, FL 32301
(904) 488-0900

Georgia
Thomas W. Hester, M.D., Acting Director
Georgia Alcohol & Drug Services Section
2 Peachtree Street NE, 4th Floor
Atlanta, GA 30309
(404) 657-6400

Guam
Marilyn L. Wingfield, Director
Department of Mental Health & Substance Abuse
P.O. Box 9400
Tamuning, GU 96911
(671) 646-9262-69

Hawaii
Elaine Wilson, Division Chief
Alcohol & Drug Abuse Division
Hawaii Department of Health
P.O. Box 3378
Honolulu, HI 96801
(808) 586-3962

Idaho
Ken Patterson, Administrator
Division of Family & Children Services
Idaho Department of Health & Welfare
450 West State Street, 3rd Floor
Boise, ID 83702
(208) 334-5935

Illinois
James E. Long, Director
Illinois Department of Alcoholism & Substance Abuse
222 South College, 2nd Floor
Springfield, IL 62704
(217) 785-9067

Indiana
John Giandelone
Deputy Director
Division of Mental Health
Contract Management
W-353, 402 W. Washington Street
Indianapolis, IN 46204-2739
(317) 232-7816

Iowa
Janet Zwick, Director
Division of Substance Abuse & Health Promotion
Iowa Department of Public Health
Lucas State Office Building
3rd Floor
Des Moines, IA 50319
(515) 281-4417

Kansas
Andrew O'Donovan, Commissioner
Kansas Alcohol & Drug Abuse Services
Biddle Building
300 Southwest Oakley
Topeka, KS 66606-1861
(913) 296-3925

Kentucky
Michael Townsend, Director
Division of Substance Abuse
Kentucky Dept. of Mental Health & Mental Retardation Services
275 East Main Street
Frankfort, KY 40621
(502) 564-2880

Louisiana
Joseph Williams, Jr.
Assistant Secretary
Office of Alcohol & Drug Abuse
Department of Health & Hospitals
1201 Capitol Access Road
P.O. Box 2790-BIN #18
Baton Rouge, LA 70821-2790
(504) 342-6717

Maine
Marlene McMullen-Pelsor
Acting Director
Office of Substance Abuse
State House Station #159
24 Stone Street
Augusta, ME 04333-0159
(207) 287-6330

Maryland
Rick Sampson, Director
Maryland State Alcohol & Drug Abuse Administration
201 West Preston Street
Baltimore, MD 21201
(410) 225-6925

Massachusetts
Dennis McCarty, Ph.D., Director
Massachusetts Division of Substance Abuse Services
150 Tremont Street
Boston, MA 02111
(617) 727-7985

Michigan
Karen Schrock, Chief
Center for Substance Abuse Services
Michigan Department of Public Health
3423 N. Logan/M.L. King Jr., Blvd.
P.O. Box 30195
Lansing, MI 48909
(517) 335-8808

Minnesota
Cynthia Turnure, Ph.D., Director
Chemical Dependency Program Division
Minnesota Department of Human Services
444 Lafayette Road
St. Paul, MN 55155-3823
(612) 296-4610

Mississippi
Anne D. Robertson, Director
Division of Alcohol and Drug Abuse
Mississippi Department of Mental Health
Robert E. Lee State Office Building
11th Floor
Jackson, MS 39201
(601) 359-1288

Missouri
Sue Giles, Director
Division of Alcohol & Drug Abuse
Missouri Department of Health
1706 East Elm Street
Jefferson City, MO 65109
(314) 751-4942

Montana
Darryl Bruno, Administrator
Alcohol & Drug Abuse Division
Department of Corrections & Human Services
1539 11th Avenue
Helena, MT 59601-1301
(406) 444-2827

Nebraska
Malcolm Heard, Director
Division of Alcoholism & Drug Abuse
Nebraska Department of Public Institutions
P.O. Box 94728
Lincoln, NE 68509-4728
(402) 471-2851, Ext. 5583

Nevada
Elizabeth Breshears, Chief
Bureau of Alcohol & Drug Abuse
Nevada Department of Human Resources
505 East King Street, Room 500
Carson City, NV 89710
(702) 687-4790

New Hampshire
Geraldine Sylvester, Director
New Hampshire Office of Alcohol & Drug Abuse Prevention
105 Pleasant Street
Concord, NH 03301
(603) 271-6119

New Jersey
Terrence O'Connor
Assistant Commissioner
Division of Alcoholism, Drug Abuse & Addiction Services
New Jersey Department of Health
CN 362
Trenton, NJ 08625-0362
(609) 292-5760

New Mexico
Geraldine Salazar, Director
Department of Health
Behavioral Health Services Division/SA
Harold Runnels Building
Room 3200 North
1190 Saint Francis Drive
Santa Fe, NM 87501
(505) 827-2601

New York
Marguerite T. Saunders
Commissioner
New York State Office of Alcoholism & Substance Abuse Services
Executive Park South, P.O. Box 8200
Albany, NY 12203
(518) 457-2061

North Carolina
Julian F. Keith, M.D., Director
Alcohol and Drug Services
North Carolina Division of Mental Health, Developmental Disabilities &
Substance Abuse Services
325 North Salisbury Street
Raleigh, NC 27611
(919) 733-4670

North Dakota
John Allen, Director
Division of Alcoholism and Drug Abuse
North Dakota Department of Human Services
Professional Building
1839 East Capitol Avenue
Bismarck, ND 58501
(701) 224-2769

Ohio
Luceille Fleming, Director
Ohio Department of Alcohol & Drug Addiction Services
Two Nationwide Plaza, 12th Floor
280 N. High Street
Columbus, OH 43215-2537
(614) 466-3445

Oklahoma
Paula Grove, Director
Substance Abuse Services
Oklahoma Department of Mental Health & Substance Abuse Services
P.O. Box 53277, Capitol Station
Oklahoma City, OK 73152-3277
(405) 271-8653

Oregon
Jeffrey N. Kushner
Office of Alcohol & Drug Abuse Programs
Department of Human Resources
1178 Chemeketa Street, NE
Room 102
Salem, OR 97310
(503) 378-2163

Pennsylvania

Jeannine Peterson, Deputy Secretary
Office of Drug & Alcohol Programs
Pennsylvania Department of Health
P.O. Box 90
Harrisburg, PA 17108
(717) 787-9857

Puerto Rico

Astrid Oyola de Benitez
Secretary Designate
Puerto Rico Department of Anti-Addiction Services
Box 21414, Rio Piedras Station
Rio Piedras, PR 00928-1414
(809) 764-3795

Rhode Island

William Pimentel, Deputy Director
Rhode Island Office of Substance Abuse
P.O. Box 20363
Cranston, RI 02920
(401) 464-2091

South Carolina

John W. Hays, Deputy Director
South Carolina Commission on Alcohol & Drug Abuse
3700 Forest Drive
Columbia, SC 29204
(803) 734-9527

South Dakota

Gilbert Sudbeck, Director
Division of Alcohol & Drug Abuse
Department of Human Services
Hillsview Plaza, East Hwy. 34
c/o 500 East Capitol
Pierre, SD 57501-5090
(605) 773-3123

Tennessee
Robbie Jackman, Assistant Commissioner
Bureau of Alcohol & Drug Abuse Services
Tennessee Department of Health
Cordell Hull Building, Room 255
Nashville, TN 37247-4401
(615) 741-1921

Texas
Bob Dickson, Executive Director
Texas Commission on Alcohol & Drug Abuse
720 Brazos Street, Suite 403
Austin, TX 78701
(512) 867-8802

Trust Territories/Pacific Islands
Masao Kumangai, M.D.
Health Services
Office of the Governor
Saipan, MP 96950
011-670-2348950

Utah
Leon PoVey, Director
Department of Social Services
Utah Division of Substance Abuse
120 North 200 West, 4th Floor
P.O. Box 45500
Salt Lake City, UT 84404
(801) 538-3939

Vermont
Steven M. Gold, Interim Director
Vermont Office of Alcohol & Drug Abuse Programs
103 South Main Street
Waterbury, VT 05676
(802) 241-2170

Virgin Islands

Laurent D. Javois, Director
Virgin Islands Division of Mental Health, Alcoholism & Drug Dependency Services
Department of Health
Charles Harwood Memorial Hospital
Christianstead, St. Croix
U.S. Virgin Islands 00820
(809) 773-1311 ext. 3013

Virginia

John F. Draude, Jr., Ph.D., Director
Office of Substance Abuse Services
Virginia Department of Mental Health, Mental Retardation & Substance Abuse Services
109 Governor Street
P.O. Box 1797
Richmond, VA 23214
(804) 786-3906

Washington

Kenneth D. Stark, Director
Division of Alcohol & Substance Abuse
Washington Department of Social & Health Services
P.O. Box 45330
Olympia, WA 98504-5330
(206) 438-8200

West Virginia

Jack C. Clohan, Jr., Director
West Virginia Division of Alcoholism & Drug Abuse
State Capitol Complex
1900 Kanawha Blvd.
Building 6, Room B-738
Charleston, WV 25305
(304) 558-2276

Wisconsin

Philip S. McCullough, Director
Bureau of Substance Abuse Services
1 West Wilson Street
P.O. Box 7851
Madison, WI 53707
(608) 266-3719

Wyoming

Harvey Hillin, Administrator
Wyoming Division of Behavioral Health
447 Hathaway Building
Cheyenne, WY 82002
(307) 777-6494

What can a person expect to find in a treatment program? What they offer may depend in part on whether it is in a residential setting (a place where people stay for a period of time), a detoxification center (a place that provides short term care while people withdraw from alcohol and drugs), or some kind of outpatient facility. The residential (inpatient) setting is the choice for a person who needs intensive and continuing help. Drug counseling, monitoring for drug use, and group support are features of many treatment programs. Designer drug users who are trying to stay drug free can help one another and be a very strong source of support. There are also programs that follow the twelve-step concept developed in Alcoholics Anonymous, and programs aimed at tearing down the defenses that designer drug users have built up to deal with the world. If you are interested in getting help with a designer drug problem, you should ask carefully about how the program works. You should also ask about the training and experience of the people who both direct and carry out the program.

While programs specifically targeted to deal with designer drugs, such as speed or ecstasy, may be hard to come by, there are some efforts being made to develop treatment programs for stimulant abuse. These drug treatment programs are typically modeled after programs designed to treat alcoholism and heroin addiction.

The initial goal in the treatment of stimulant abuse, whether it is a member of the amphetamine family or cocaine, is to stop the use of the drug. Counseling and support services provided by the drug treatment program should be helpful in achieving this objective. In addition, there are a number of practical strategies which may be useful in helping a person stay drug free. Frank Gawin and Everett Ellinwood, Jr., suggest that steps should be taken to minimize the patient's exposure to people and situations that encourage designer drug use. These steps may include limiting access to money, limiting social activities, and having a family member or friend monitor the patient during periods of high craving for the drug.

Once the goal of staying away from designer drugs has been achieved, the emphasis should shift to preventing relapse. This goal is very important because relapse rates for drug abuse are often high. Gawin and Ellinwood offer a number of ideas which may be helpful here. They suggest that recovering drug abusers should be aware of the kinds of situations where the risk of relapse is high so they can steer clear of them. They should also practice avoidance strategies, socialize with people who do not use drugs, strengthen memories of the negative consequences of drugs, reduce stress in their lives, and make needed lifestyle changes.

One of the reasons for relapse—even after what appears to be successful treatment—is that episodes of craving for designer drugs can occur for a long time after stopping the drug. As is true for most substance abuse problems, staying away from designer drugs is likely to be a long-term problem. Most designer drugs are seductive and it is no easy task for a person to stay free of them once he or she has developed a dependency on them.

Treatment for designer drug abuse can be difficult. Relapses are all too frequent. It makes a lot of sense to try to avoid designer drug abuse in the first place. Drug education is one of the keys to doing this. Many communities have moved ahead and developed drug education programs, which are often carried out in the schools. Some communities, for example, have established DARE (Drug Abuse Resistance Education) programs in which police officers spend a lot of time working directly with young children in the schools. There is no lack of creative ideas for coming up with drug education programs in this country. Two of these programs are described here. The concepts in these programs may help stimulate ideas for drug prevention programs in your own schools and communities.

A team of researchers led by Yale University's Marlene Caplan has been working with middle grade students in south central Connecticut. During a twenty-session program, they not only present information about drugs, such as designer drugs, but they also teach the students how to deal better with the stress of early adolescence. They help set goals for healthy living, teach problem-solving skills and give assertiveness training to help in resisting peer pressure. This combination of drug information

Many communities have established Drug Abuse Resistance Education (DARE) programs in which police officers spend a lot of time working directly with young people in schools, to try to keep them from ever getting involved with illegal drugs.

and personal development is an interesting and promising approach to drug prevention.

Arthur Safer and Carol Harding have been working with high-risk Chicago junior high and high school students. Their approach to drug prevention involves live theater performances relating to drug abuse. After a performance, the students become involved both with discussion and role-playing. A believable and well-performed drama can touch emotions and focus attention on a serious problem. The Chicago program, which has reached over a thousand young people, suggests that theater can be another tool in community efforts at drug prevention.

While staying away from designer drugs is a personal decision—a matter of each person taking responsibility for his or her own actions—it is a decision that all of us can help influence. As friends and family members, we can make it clear that we do not place a positive value on drug use of any kind and that we see such behavior as unwise, unproductive, and risky. We can show by example that there are better ways to live life. As a community, we can offer sound drug prevention programs that not only offer the facts about designer drugs in a credible way, but also help strengthen the resolve of young people to stay clear of designer drugs.

Questions For Discussion

1. If you had a friend who was trying to stop using a designer drug but was having trouble doing so, what things would you tell him or her to help?

2. What could you tell someone about the drug treatment services that are available in your community?

3. Why do you think that many people who manage to stop using designer drugs return to drug use after a period of time?

Chapter Notes

Introduction

1. Paul R. Robbins, *Problems and Treatment of Heroin Addiction in the United States*, Leonia, N.J.: Behavioral Science Tape Library, Sigma Information, 1974, Side 1.

2. Keiichi Yamamoto et al., "3 Fatalities After Communal Use of Methamphetamine," *Archiv fur Kriminologie* 188, September–October 1991, pp. 72–76.

Chapter 1

1. Henderson's view was cited in Terra Ziporyn, "A Growing Industry and Menace: Makeshift Laboratory's Designer Drugs," *Journal of the American Medical Association* 256, December 12, 1986, p. 3061.

2. These drawings are modeled after drawings presented by Robert J. Roberton before a United States Senate Subcommittee. Report of the Hearing Before the Senate Subcommittee on Children, Family, Drugs, and Alcoholism on Designer Drugs, July 25, 1985, p. 21.

3. In testimony before the Senate Subcommittee on designer drugs, Dr. Donald I. MacDonald suggested that the number of possible fentanyl analogs would be in the thousands. "In the case of fentanyl, there are at least 4,000 possible analogs which can be produced, and it does not take a genius to do it." Senate Subcommittee report, July 25, 1985, p. 36.

Chapter 2

1. Michelle McCormick, *Designer-Drug Abuse*, New York: Watts, 1989, Chapter 2.

2. J.M. Wright et al., "Chronic Parkinsonism Secondary to Intranasal Administration of a Product of Meperdine—Analogue Synthesis," *New England Journal of Medicine* 310, February 2, 1984, p. 325.

3. Senate Subcommittee Report on Designer Drugs, p. 13.

4. John P. Morgan et al., "Duplicitous Drugs: The History and Recent Status of Look-alike Drugs," *Journal of Psychoactive Drugs* 19, January–March 1987, pp. 21–23.

5. Brent T. Burton, "Heavy Metal and Organic Contaminants Associated with Illicit Methamphetamine Production," *Methamphetamine Abuse: Epidemiologic Issues and Implications*, eds., Marissa A. Miller and Nicholas J. Kozel, Rockville, Md.: NIDA, 1991, p. 48.

6. *Physicians Desk Reference*, Montvale, N.J.: Medical Economics Data, 1993, pp. 1002–1003.

7. Hiroshi Suwaki, "Methamphetamine Abuse in Japan," *Methamphetamine Abuse: Epidemiologic Issues and Implications*, pp. 84–98 and Byung In Cho, "Trends and Patterns of Methamphetamine Abuse in the Republic of Korea," *Methamphetamine Abuse: Epidemiologic Issues and Implications*, pp. 99–108.

8. "Methamphetamine Abuse," *NIDA Capsules*, Rockville, Md.: NIDA, January 1990, p. 1.

9. Ibid.

10. Burton, pp. 54–55.

11. S. Tohhara, A. Kato, and T. Nakajima, "Methamphetamine Abuse by Smoking," *Arukoru Kenkyuto Yakubutsu Ison* 25, 1990, pp. 467–474.

12. C. Edgar Cook, "Pyrolytic Characteristics, Pharmacokinetics, and Bioavailability of Smoked Heroin, Cocaine, Phencyclidine, and Methamphetamine." In *Methamphetamine Abuse: Epidemiologic Issues and Implications*, p. 18.

13. "Methamphetamine Abuse," *NIDA Capsules*, p. 2.

14. Ibid.

15. Klaus A. Miczek and Jennifer W. Tidey, "Amphetamines: Aggressive and Social Behavior." In *Pharmacology and Toxicology of Amphetamine and Related Designer Drugs*, eds., Khursheed Asghar and Erol DeSouza, Rockville, Md.: NIDA, 1989, p. 90.

16. Everett H. Ellinwood, Jr., "Assault and Homicide Associated with Amphetamine Abuse," *American Journal of Psychiatry* 127, March 1971, p. 1174.

17. Ibid. pp. 1171-1172.

18. Paul R. Robbins, "Heroin Addicts' Views of Commonly Abused Drugs: A Semantic Differential Approach," *Journal of Personality Assessment* 36, August 1972, p. 368. The semantic differential technique is described in detail in Charles E. Osgood, George J. Suci, and Percy H. Tannenbaum, *The Measurement of Meaning*, Urbana, IL.: University of Illinois Press, 1957.

19. Marissa A. Miller, "Trends and Patterns of Methamphetamine Smoking in Hawaii," In *Methamphetamine Abuse: Epidemiologic Issues and Implications*, pp. 78–79.

Chapter 3

1. Ken Liska, *The Pharmacist's Guide to the Most Misused and Abused Drugs in America*, New York: Collier, 1988, p. 123.

2. Ibid.

3. Joseph Downing, "The Physiological and Psychological Effects of MDMA on Normal Volunteers," *Journal of Psychoactive Drugs* 18, October–December 1986, p. 336.

4. The reports of ecstasy users are taken from two studies. These are the study cited by Downing, and one by George Greer and Requa Tolbert, "Subjective Reports of the Effects of MDMA in a Clinical Setting," *Journal of Psychoactive Drugs* 18, October–December 1986, pp. 319–327. A questionnaire study of 100 ecstasy users carried out by N. Solowij reported similar findings. In Solowij's study, major effects of using the drug were a positive mood, feelings of intimacy, and closeness to others. N. Solowij, W. Hall, and N. Lee "Recreational MDMA Use in Sydney: A Profile of 'Ecstasy' Users and Their Experiences with the Drug," *British Journal of Addictions* 87, August 1992, pp. 1161–1172.

5. "MDMA," *NIDA Capsules*, Rockville, Md.: NIDA, July 1985, pp. 1–2.

6. Stefano Pallanti and Donatella Mazzi, "MDMA (Ecstasy) Precipitation of Panic Disorder," *Biological Psychiatry* 32, July 1992, pp. 91–95.

7. Marjory Roberts, "MDMA: Madness, not Ecstasy," *Psychology Today*, June 1986, p. 14.

8. Francis J. Creighton, Dawn L. Black, and Clive E. Hyde, "Ecstasy Psychosis and Flashbacks," *British Journal of Psychiatry* 159, 1991, pp. 713–715.

9. John H. Krystal et al., "Chronic 3,4-Methylenedioxymethamphetamine (MDMA) Use: Effects on Mood and Neuropsychological Function" *American Journal of Drug and Alcohol Abuse* 18, September 1992, pp. 331–341.

10. Paul R. Robbins, *Understanding Depression*, Jefferson, N.C.: McFarland, 1993, pp. 46–48.

11. Teri Randall, "Ecstasy-Fueled 'Rave' Parties Become Dances of Death for English Youths," *Journal of the American Medical Association* 268, September 23, 1992, p. 1505.

12. Teri Randall, "'Rave' Scene, Ecstasy Use, Leap Atlantic," *Journal of the American Medical Association* 268, September 23, 1992, p. 1506.

13. Report of the Senate Subcommittee on Designer Drugs, p. 18.

14. Ibid.

15. Ibid., p. 24.

16. Ibid., p. 59.

17. Jonathan Hibbs, Joshua Perper, and Charles L. Winek, "An Outbreak of Designer Drug-related Deaths in Pennsylvania," *Journal of the American Medical Association* 265, February 27, 1991, pp. 1011–1013.

18. A discussion of emergency room treatment of Fentanyl analog overdose is presented in David A. Jerrard, "'Designer Drugs'—A Current Perspective," *Journal of Emergency Medicine* 8, November–December 1990, p. 737.

Chapter 4

1. Edward Kaufman, "The Applications of Biological Vulnerability Research to Drug Abuse Prevention," In *Biological Vulnerability to Drug Abuse*, p. 175.

2. This is an old notion in psychology. It was once called the law of effect. Much of the research on the effects of reinforcement on behavior was carried out by the late B.F. Skinner and his followers.

3. Paul R. Robbins, *Marijuana: A Short Course. Update for the Eighties*, Brookline Village, Mass.: Branden, 1983, pp. 29–35.

4. Michelle McCormick, *Designer-Drug Abuse*, New York: Watts, 1989, p. 54.

5. Ibid, p. 55.

6. Paul R. Robbins and Roland H. Tanck, "A Factor Analysis of Coping Behavior," *Journal of Clinical Psychology* 34, April 1978, p. 380.

7. Jill Novaceck, Robert Raskin, and Robert Hogan, "Why do Adolescents Use Drugs? Age, Sex and User Differences," *Journal of Youth and Adolescence* 20, October 1991, pp. 475–492.

8. A discussion of personality tendencies associated with substance abuse is presented in David M. Murray and Cheryl L. Perry, "The Prevention of Adolescent Drug Abuse: Implications of Etiological, Developmental, Behavioral and Environmental Models." In *Etiology of Drug Abuse: Implications for Prevention*, eds., Coryl L. Jones and Robert J. Battjes, Rockville, Md.: NIDA, 1985, pp. 236–256.

Chapter 5

1. J. David Hawkins, Denise M. Lishner, and Richard F. Catalano, Jr., "Childhood Predictors and the Prevention of Adolescent Substance Abuse." In *Etiology of Drug Abuse*, p. 81.

2. Ibid.

3. Patricia J. Bush and Ronald J. Iannotti, "The Development of Children's Health Orientations and Behaviors: Lessons for Substance Use Prevention." In *Etiology of Drug Abuse: Implications for Prevention*, p. 58.

4. Ibid.

5. Ibid.

6. Judith S. Brook et al., "African-American and Puerto Rican Drug Use: Personality, Familial and Other Environmental Risk Factors," *Genetic, Social, and General Psychology Monographs* 118, November 1992, p. 428.

7. Bush and Iannotti, p. 57.

8. Leo Shilts, "The Relationship of Early Adolescent Substance Use to Extracurricular Activities, Peer Influence and Personal Attitudes," *Adolescence* 26, Fall 1991, p. 615.

9. Brook, p. 428.

10. "Methamphetamine Abuse," *NIDA Capsules*, p. 2. The cost of an equal amount of cocaine was $100.

11. Marissa A. Miller, "Trends and patterns of Methamphetamine Smoking in Hawaii," *Methamphetamine Abuse: Empidemiologic Issues and Implications*, p. 79.

12. Paul R. Robbins and Julius F. Nugent, III, "Perceived Consequences of Addiction: A Comparison Between Alcoholics and Heroin-addicted Patients," *Journal of Clinical Psychology* 31, April 1975, Table 1, p. 368.

Chapter 6

1. Brent T. Burton, "Heavy Metal and Organic Contaminants Associated with Illicit Methamphetamine Production," *Methamphetamine: Abuse Epidemiologic Issues and Implications*, Marissa A. Miller and Nicholas J. Kozel, eds., Rockville, Md.: NIDA, 1991, p. 48.

2. Amy Goldstein, "The Young in D.C. Meet Drugs Early," *Washington Post*, August 31, 1993, p. 1.

3. Robert Raskin, Jill Novaceck, and Robert Hogan, "Drug Culture, Expertise and Substance Use," *Journal of Youth and Adolescence* 21, October 1992, p. 635.

4. *Drug Abuse and Drug Abuse Research*, Rockville, Md.: Alcohol Drug Abuse and Mental Health Administration, 1991, p. 27.

5. Ibid, p. 25.

6. David E. Moody et al., "Mandatory Post Accident Drug and Alcohol Testing for the Federal Railroad Administration (FRA)." In *Drugs in the Workplace: Research and Evaluation Data*, eds., Steven W. Gust, J. Michael Walsh, Linda B. Thomas and Dennis J. Crouch, Vol. 2, Rockville, Md.: NIDA, 1990, pp. 79–96.

7. Gary D. Irvine and Ling Chin, "The Environmental Impact and Adverse Health Effects of the Clandestine Manufacture of Methamphetamine," In *Methamphetamine Abuse: Epidemiologic Issues and Implications*, p. 37.

8. Ibid.

9. Ibid., p. 33.

10. "Update on Methcathinone or 'Cat,'" *Drug Abuse Update*, Winter 1993, pp. 12–13.

11. Senate Subcommittee Report on Designer Drugs, p. 76.

Chapter 7

1. George L. Sternbach and Joseph Varon, "'Designer Drugs.' Recognizing and Managing Their Toxic Effects. 'Adam,' 'Eve,' 'Ecstasy,' 'China White,'" *Postgraduate Medicine* 91, June 1992, pp. 175–176.

2. Jerrard, pp. 733–741.

3. Ibid, p. 739.

Bibliography

Baumrind, Diana. "Familial Antecedents of Adolescent Drug Use: A Developmental Perspective." In *Etiology of Drug Abuse: Implications for Prevention*, eds., Coryl L. Jones and Robert J. Battjes , Rockville, MD: NIDA, 1985, pp. 13–44.

Brook, Judith S., Martin Whiteman, Elinor B. Balka, and Beatrix A. Hamburg, "African-American and Puerto Rican Drug Use: Personality, Familial and Other Environmental Risk Factors." *Genetic, Social and General Psychology Monographs* 118, November 1992, pp. 417–438.

Burton, Brent T. "Heavy Metal and Organic Contaminants Associated with Illicit Methamphetamine Production." In *Methamphetamine Abuse: Epidemiologic Issues and Implications*, eds., Marissa A. Miller and Nicholas J. Kozel, Rockville, Md.: NIDA, 1991, pp. 47–59.

Bush, Patricia J. and Ronald J. Iannotti. "The Development of Children's Health Orientations and Behaviors: Lessons for Substance Use Prevention." In *Etiology of Drug Abuse: Implications for Prevention*, eds., Coryl L. Jones and Robert J. Battjes, Rockville, Md.: NIDA, 1985, pp. 45–74.

Caplan, Marlene, et al. "Social Competence Promotion with Inner-city and Suburban Young Adolescents: Effects on Social Adjustment and Alcohol Use." *Journal of Consulting and Clinical Psychology* 60, February 1992, pp. 56–63.

Cho, Byung I. "Trends and Patterns of Methamphetamine Abuse in the Republic of Korea." In *Methamphetamine Abuse: Epidemiologic Issues and Implications*, eds., Marissa A. Miller and Nicholas J. Kozel, Rockville, Md.: NIDA, 1991, pp. 99–108.

Cook, C. Edgar. "Pyrolytic Characteristics, Pharmacokinetics, and Bioavailability of Smoked Heroin, Cocaine, Phencyclidine, and Methamphetamine." In *Methamphetamine Abuse: Epidemiologic Issues and Implications*, eds., Marissa A. Miller and Nicholas J. Kozel , Rockville, Md.: NIDA, 1991, pp. 6–23.

Creighton, Francis J., Dawn L. Black, and Clive E. Hyde. "Ecstasy Psychosis and Flashbacks." *British Journal of Psychiatry* 159, 1991, pp. 713–715.

Downing, Joseph. "The Physiological and Psychological Effects of MDMA on Normal Volunteers." *Journal of Psychoactive Drugs* 18, October–December 1986, p. 335–340.

Drug Abuse and Drug Abuse Research. The third triennial report from the secretary, Department of Health and Human Services. Rockville, Md.: Alcohol Drug Abuse and Mental Health Administration, 1991.

Ellinwood, Everett H., Jr. "Assault and Homicide Associated with Amphetamine Abuse." *American Journal of Psychiatry* 127, March 1971, pp. 1170–1175.

Gawin, Frank H. and Everett H. Ellinwood, Jr. "Cocaine and Other Stimulants: Actions, Abuse, and Treatment." *New England Journal of Medicine* 318, May 5, 1988, pp. 1173–1182.

Goldstein, Amy. "The Young in D.C. Meet Drugs Early." *Washington Post*, August 31, 1993, p. 1.

Greer, George and Requa Tolbert, "Subjective Reports of the Effects of MDMA in a Clinical Setting." *Journal of Psychoactive Drugs* 18, October–December 12, 1986, pp. 319–327.

Hawkins, J. David, Denise M. Lishner, and Richard F. Catalano, Jr. "Childhood Predictors and the Prevention of Adolescent Substance Abuse." In *Etiology of Drug Abuse: Implications for Prevention*, eds., Coryl L. Jones and Robert J. Battjes, Rockville, Md.: NIDA, 1985, pp. 75–126.

Hibbs, Jonathan, Joshua Perper, and Charles L. Winek. "An Outbreak of Designer Drug-related Deaths in Pennsylvania." *Journal of the American Medical Association* 265, February 27, 1991, pp. 1011–1013.

Irvine, Gary D. and Ling Chin. "The Environmental Impact and Adverse Health Effects of the Clandestine Manufacture of Methamphetamine." In *Methamphetamine Abuse: Epidemiologic Issues and Implications*, eds., Marissa A. Miller and Nicholas J. Kozel, Rockville, Md.: NIDA, 1991, pp. 33–46.

Jerrard, David A. "'Designer Drugs'—A Current Perspective." *Journal of Emergency Medicine* 8, November–December 1990, pp. 733–741.

Kafka, Randy R. and Perry London. "Communication in Relationships and Adolescent Substance Use: The Influence of Parents and Friends." *Adolescence* 26, Fall 1991, pp. 587–598.

Kaufman, Edward. "The Applications of Biological Vulnerability Research to Drug Abuse Prevention." In *Biological Vulnerability to Drug Abuse*, eds., Roy W. Pickens and Dace S. Svikis, Rockville, Md.: NIDA, 1988, pp. 174–180.

Krystal, John H., et al. "Chronic 3, 4-Methylenedioxymethamphetamine (MDMA) Use: Effects on Mood and Neuropsychological Function?" *American Journal of Drug and Alcohol Abuse* 18, September 1992, pp. 331–341.

Liska, Ken. *The Pharmacist's Guide to the Most Misused and Abused Drugs in America.* New York: Collier, 1988.

McCormick, Michelle. *Designer-Drug Abuse.* New York: Watts, 1989.

"MDMA." *NIDA Capsules*, Rockville, Md.: NIDA, 1985.

"Methamphetamine Abuse." *NIDA Capsules*, Rockville, Md.: NIDA, January 1990.

Miczek, Klaus A. and Jennifer W. Tidey. "Amphetamines: Aggressive and Social Behavior." In *Pharmacology and Toxicology of Amphetamine and Related Designer Drugs*, eds., Khursheed Asghar and Erol DeSouza, Rockville, Md.: NIDA, 1989, pp. 68–100.

Miller, Marissa A. "Trends and Patterns of Methamphetamine Smoking in Hawaii." In *Methamphetamine Abuse: Epidemiologic Issues and Implications*, eds., Marissa A. Miller and Nicholas J. Kozel, Rockville, Md.: NIDA, 1991, pp. 72–83.

Moody, David E., et al. "Mandatory Post Accident Drug and Alcohol Testing for the Federal Railroad Administration (FRA)." In *Drugs in the Workplace: Research and Evaluation Data*, eds., Steven W. Gust, J. Michael Walsh, Linda B. Thomas and Dennis J. Crouch, Vol. 2, Rockville, Md.: NIDA, 1990, pp. 79–96.

Morgan, John R., et al. "Duplicitous Drugs: The History and Recent Status of Look-alike Drugs." *Journal of Psychoactive Drugs* 19, January–March 1987, pp. 21–31.

Murray, David M. and Cheryl L. Perry. "The Prevention of Adolescent Drug Abuse: Implications of Etiological, Developmental, Behavioral and Environmental Models." In *Etiology of Drug Abuse: Implications for Prevention*, eds., Coryl L. Jones and Robert J. Battjes, Rockville, Md.: NIDA, 1985, pp. 236–256.

National Directory of Drug Abuse and Alcoholism Treatment and Prevention Programs, Rockville, Md. Substance Abuse and Mental Health Services Administration, 1992.

Novacek, Jill, Robert Raskin, and Robert Hogan. "Why do Adolescents Use Drugs? Age, Sex and User Differences." *Journal of Youth and Adolescence* 20, October 1991, pp. 475–492.

Osgood, Charles E., George J. Suci, and Percy H. Tannenbaum. *The Measurement of Meaning*. Urbana, Ill.: University of Illinois Press, 1957.

Pallanti, Stefano and Donatella Mazzi. "MDMA (Ecstasy) Precipitation of Panic Disorder." *Biological Psychiatry* 32, July 1992, pp. 91–95.

Physicians Desk Reference, Montvale, N.J.: Medical Economics Data, 1993.

Pickens, Roy W., and Dace S. Svikis. "Genetic Vulnerability to Drub Abuse." In *Biological Vulnerability to Drug Abuse*, eds., Roy W. Pickens and Dace S. Svikis, Rockville, Md.: NIDA, 1988, pp. 1–8.

Pickens, Roy W. and Dace S. Svikis. "The Twin Method in the Study of Vulnerability to Drug Abuse." In *Biological Vulnerability to Drug Abuse*, eds., Roy W. Pickens and Dace S. Svikis, Rockville, Md.: NIDA, 1988, pp. 41–51.

Randall, Teri. "Ecstasy-Fueled 'Rave' Parties Become Dances of Death for English Youths." *Journal of the American Medical Association* 268, September 23, 1992, pp. 1505–1506.

Randall, Teri. "'Rave' Scene, Ecstasy Use, Leap Atlantic." *Journal of the American Medical Association* 268, September 23, 1992, pp. 1505–1506.

Raskin, Robert, Jill Novacek, and Robert Hogan. "Drug Culture, Expertise and Substance Use." *Journal of Youth and Adolescence* 21, October 1992, pp. 625–637.

Report of the Hearing Before the Senate Subcommittee on Children, Family, Drugs and Alcoholism on Designer Drugs, July 25, 1985. Washington, D.C. Government Printing Office.

Robbins, Paul R. *Marijuana: A Short Course. Update for the Eighties.* Brookline Village, Mass.: Branden, 1983.

Roberts, Marjory. "MDMA: Madness, not Ecstasy." *Psychology Today,* June 1986, pp. 14–15.

Safer, Arthur L. and Carol G. Harding. "Under Pressure Program: Using Live Theatre to Investigate Adolescents' Attitudes and Behavior Related to Drug and Alcohol Abuse Education and Prevention." *Adolescence* 28, Spring 1993, pp. 135–148.

Schafer, John and Sandra A. Brown. "Marijuana and Cocaine Effect Expectancies and Drug Use Patterns." *Journal of Consulting and Clinical Psychology* 59, August 1991, pp. 558–565.

Shilts, Leo. "The Relationship of Early Adolescent Substance Use to Extracurricular Activities, Peer Influence and Personal Attitudes." *Adolescence* 26, Fall 1991, pp. 613–617.

Solowij, N., W. Hall, and N. Lee. "Recreational MDMA Use in Sydney: A Profile of 'Ecstasy' Users and Their Experiences with the Drug." *British Journal of Addictions* 87, August 1992, pp. 1161–1172.

Sternbach, George L. and Joseph Varon. "'Designer Drugs.' Recognizing and Managing Their Toxic Effects." *Postgraduate Medicine* 91, June 1992, pp. 165–171.

Suwaki, Hiroshi. "Methamphetamine Abuse in Japan." In *Methamphetamine Abuse: Epidemiologic Issues and Implications*, eds., Marissa A. Miller and Nicholas J. Kozel, Rockville, Md.: NIDA, 1991, pp. 84–98.

Tohhara, S., A. Kato, and T. Nakajima. "Methamphetamine Abuse by Smoking." *Arukoru Kenkyuto Yakubutsu Ison* 25, 1990, pp. 467–474.

"Update on Methcathinone or 'Cat.'" *Drug Abuse Update*, Winter 1993, pp. 12–13.

Wright, J.M., R.A. Wall, Thomas L. Perry, and D.W. Paty. "Chronic Parkinsonism Secondary to Intranasal Administration of a Product of Meperidine-analogue Synthesis." *New England Journal of Medicine* 310, February 2, 1984, p. 325.

Glossary

alpha-methyl fentanyl—The first illegal fentanyl analog sold on the streets. It is a simple alteration of fentanyl and is about two hundred times as potent as morphine.

Benzedrine[TM]—A name for amphetamine that may be prescribed by physicians. It comes in capsules or tablets. It may be called "bennies" on the street.

carfentanyl—A legally produced analog of fentanyl used in the capture of wild animals.

China White—A street name for pure heroin from Southeast Asia. Fentanyl analogs are often sold under this name.

designer drugs— These are drugs synthesized in laboratories that produce psychoactive effects similar to drugs that are controlled substances and are sold on the street. Designer drugs are made by slightly altering the chemical structure of an existing drug.

Dexedrine[TM]—An amphetamine that may be prescribed by physicians. It comes in an a liquid or tablets. On the street, it may be called "dexies."

drug culture—This is a subculture within the larger society where buying, selling, and using illegal drugs is an important part of everyday life.

ecstasy—A street name for the drug 3,4-methylenedioxymethamphetamine (MDMA). The drug is derived from MDA and is chemically similar to methamphetamine. Ecstasy has both stimulant and hallucinogenic properties.

fentanyl—A synthetic short-acting narcotic widely used in surgery.

ice—A name given to methamphetamine that comes in the form of a large clear crystal of high purity. It is usually smoked in a glass pipe.

MPTP—A substance that is produced when errors are made in the synthesis of MPPP, an analog to the narcotic meperidine. It causes symptoms like those of Parkinson's disease.

meperidine—A synthetic narcotic sold under the trade name Demerol.^{TM} The drug has a shorter action than morphine.

methamphetamine—The drug is a member of the amphetamine family. The drug is a psychostimulant that produces feelings of euphoria when injected or smoked.

narcotic—A drug that is derived from opium or a substance like opium. It controls pain. However, the drug creates dependence. Some newer narcotics such as meperidine are synthetic.

neurotoxin—Any agent which is destructive to cells in the nervous system and brain.

psychoactive—Drugs that alter a person's thinking, perceptions, and emotions are called psychoactive drugs.

psychosis—A serious mental disorder often marked by disturbances in reality contact. Symptoms may include delusions and hallucinations.

serotonin—A chemical that plays an important role in the transmission of messages within the brain and through the nervous system. Such chemicals are called neurotransmitters.

speed—A street name for methamphetamine. It is also known by such names as "crank" and "go fast."

synthetic analogs—Drugs produced in the laboratory. Their chemical structures are slightly altered from existing drugs.

tolerance—Reduction of a person's response to a drug following repeated use.

Index

A

Adam, 31
amphetamine, 17-21, 24-27, 50,
   66, 68, 69

B

Benzadrine ^{TM,} 18
Biphetamine ^{TM}, 19, 20

C

CAT, 72
china white, 11, 13, 40, 42, 46, 68
cocaine, 8, 69, 70
crank, 21
crystal, 8

D

Dexedrine ^{TM}, 18
drug culture, 66-67
drug use, legal, 65-66

E

ecstasy, 12, 31-40, 46, 50, 51, 72,
   92
   dose levels of, 32-33
   effects of, 33-38, 50, 51
   rave parties and, 38-40

F

family relationships, 56-63
fentanyl, 10-11, 40-42, 43
fentanyl analogs, 11, 12-13, 40-44,
   46, 68, 72, 74, 78

H

heredity and drug abuse, 4

heroin, 8, 9, 63, 69-70

I

ice, 8, 27-29, 46, 47, 62, 63, 69, 77

L

laboratories, 12, 70-72

M

MDA, 32
MDMA, 31-33
MPPP, 16, 109
MPTP, 12, 15-17, 46, 109
marijuana, 9, 50, 60, 62
meperidine, 16
methamphetamine, 6-8, 17,
   21-23, 69, 78
   duration, 22
   effects, 21-23
   injection vs. smoking, 7, 22
mexican brown, 42
moivations for drug use, 49-52

N

narcotics, 10, 43

P

Parkinson's Disease, drug use and,
   16
peer relationships, drug use and,
   61-62
personality, 52-54
pollution, drugs and, 70
prevention programs, 93-95

R

relapse, prevention of, 92-93

S

speed, *see also* methamphetamine, 8, 12, 17, 46, 69, 72, 77, 92
state drug enforcement offices, 78-91
synthetic analogs, 10

T

treatment programs, 91-93

V

values, drug use and, 61

X

XTC, 31